A Guide to Professional Development for Graduate Students in English

A Guide to Professional Development for Graduate Students in English

Cindy Moore
Eastern Kentucky University

Hildy Miller
Portland State University

National Council of Teachers of English
1111 W. Kenyon Road, Urbana, Illinois 61801–1096

Staff Editor: Bonny Graham

Manuscript Editor: Amy Bauman

Interior Design: Pat Mayer

Cover Design: Frank P. Cucciarre, Blink Concept & Design, Inc.

Cover Photo: Blend Images, LLC

NCTE Stock Number: 19235

Library of Congress Cataloging-in-Publication Data

Moore, Cindy, 1963–
    A guide to professional development for graduate students in English / Cindy Moore, Hildy Miller.
            p.   cm.
        ISBN-13: 978-0-8141-1923-5 ((pbk))
    1. College teachers—United States. 2. English teachers—United States.
3. Professional socialization—United States. I. Miller, Hildy, 1950–   II. Title.
LB1778.2.M66 2006
428.0071'5—dc22

                                                                2006024664

Contents

Acknowledgments

W e are indebted to the following people for making this project possible: Zarina Hock, our editor, for her enthusiastic support throughout our research and writing process; our anonymous reviewers for their encouragement and insights; and the many colleagues and friends, both in our departments and located across the country, who provided us with inspiration, information, and helpful feedback. Tim Houghton, Peggy O'Neill, and Suzette Henke offered especially thorough responses to early drafts and revisions, and for that we are particularly grateful. Finally, we want to thank all of the graduate students we have advised and all of our professional mentors. Without them, this guide could not have been imagined.

Introduction

I f you are like most English majors, you became fascinated years ago with all aspects of the English language. You were likely the child who read books under the bed covers with a flashlight long after lights were supposed to be out. Or, you can distinctly recall writing a poem practically as soon as you were able to write at all. As time went on, you were the one who started a neighborhood newsletter, writing advice columns and seeking articles and artwork from friends. In your under-graduate years, you were likely drawn inexorably to English, enjoying the challenges of reading varied literature, discovering critical theory, studying the rhetorical and linguistic structures of language, and developing your talents at critical or creative writing. And then graduate school beckoned with its promise of spending even more time pursuing this lifelong compelling interest.

Yet, somewhere along the way, you also likely began to wonder how to make a living out of your fascination and facility with language. After all, majoring in English does not lead down the sort of straight career path that students follow when they plan to be doctors, lawyers, or engineers. To answer your questions about career possibilities, you may have attended workshops in which new faculty tried to articulate how they succeeded in a tough academic job market when others didn't. Or, at these same workshops, you may have listened to former English majors talk about how they parlayed their course work into rewarding careers in editing, writing, and administration. How did they do it? Many of them will attribute their good fortune to blind luck—and luck is certainly a part of the career path in any field. However, many others will identify ways in which they consciously took control of their career paths by becoming professionalized. That is, they learned the ropes of their chosen field as quickly as possible and assumed a dual identity as both student and member of the profession. And, by doing so, they significantly increased both their odds of landing a good job and their chances for successfully handling new professional responsibilities.

While early success in any career can hinge on quality education and training, there is growing recognition that the professionalization experiences obtained in graduate school are especially crucial for students seeking continuing, full-time (i.e., tenure-track) faculty positions. As evidence of the situation, Robert Boice, a national leader in faculty development studies, estimates that only 3–5 percent of new faculty members are "quick starters," that is, able to perform professionally at exemplary levels in their first few years without help (5). The rest often flounder, largely because of an underlying assumption on everyone's part—the current institutions, the new faculty members, and their former graduate programs—that somewhere and somehow faculty have already learned what they need to know in order to succeed on the job. Besimon, Ward, and Sanders explain this disconnect: ". . . [S]tudies of tenure-track faculty have revealed that there is an unstated assumption that newcomers to the profession know how to accomplish what is expected of them. The reality, however, is that new faculty who have a clear idea of how to structure their roles in order to survive the probationary period appear to be the exception" (xvii). What is this knowledge—these tacit rules of the game? Specialists in faculty development call this knowledge "socialization," which Robert Mercer characterizes as "the process by which individuals acquire the values, attitudes, norms, knowledge, and skills needed to exist in a given society" (Schoenfeld and Magnan 37). For someone on the tenure track in English, having this knowledge can mean writing a dissertation that can be readily converted into a book or set of articles or possessing the administrative experience to run a writing program efficiently while still writing and teaching. It can mean knowing how to negotiate with colleagues on committees to achieve goals and avoid conflicts or how to balance professional responsibilities with the personal demands of self, friends, and family. For the variety of nonacademic careers that English majors choose—in business, nonprofit organizations, and technical companies—having the knowledge that will make an individual a quick starter is equally important because of the tough, competitive economy in which we find ourselves today.

Most graduate programs do their best to provide practical experiences that coincide with what they envision their students eventually doing. Many English programs, for example, offer teaching assistantships with accompanying practicums and faculty mentors willing to guide students through substantive scholarly projects. However, even these efforts may fall short of the socialization that is actually needed, such as how to establish oneself as a teacher, scholar, and, in many cases, an administrator; how to seek out the resources crucial to achieve in these areas; how to network professionally in and outside the field of English; and, for those pursuing university careers, how to navigate the murky waters of academic politics. Besimon, Ward, and Sanders observe: "Unfortunately, many graduate programs do not address their students' next professional step after completion of their degree. Graduate training is simply inadequate preparation for understanding academic culture and the demands of a faculty position" (50–51). Why does this gap persist? One prime reason is that graduate programs often feel stretched by the tension of trying to provide both scholarly and professional preparation for students. It may take a major investment of a program's time and resources just to offer a full spectrum of graduate courses. Correspondingly, graduate students may also find most of their energies devoted to succeeding in those intellectually engaging courses. With so much attention focused on the curriculum, both faculty and students may be hard pressed to take on much more. Yet, it is often at extracurricular activities for professional development, such as informal lunches or workshops, that graduate students get the socialization necessary to succeed later in their careers.

Nowadays, this socialization is necessary not only to succeed in a career but also, even more urgently, to land a job in the first place. Recent surveys indicate that a mere 40 percent of new PhDs in English will attain tenure-track positions right out of graduate school (Laurence 14–15). Nationwide hiring freezes, a marked diminution in the overall numbers of tenure-track jobs, and radical changes in the English discipline itself and its role in the academy have increased market pressures. Career paths in nonacademic jobs may be even harder to negotiate, as even less advice is readily available. As a result, our notions of what graduate programs and students must do has changed. Whereas once graduate school was a distinct scholarly experience separate from the careers for which it prepared students, today the lines that distinguish graduate students from assistant professors are blurred. Dissertations become books, the teaching of introductory courses becomes the teaching of more sophisticated discipline-specific courses, and the administrative experience of staffing writing courses becomes the process of running an entire writing program. Adroitly managing one's own dissertation committee can turn rather quickly into skillfully managing committees for one's students or collaborative projects for nonacademic jobs. The grant a graduate student pursued, the conference presentation idea submitted, the textbook selection committee served on—all of these professional experiences bridge graduate school and the academic or nonacademic career that follows. "What it once took for an assistant professor to get tenure," many faculty tell their graduate students, "it now takes for a graduate student to get a job as an assistant professor." These accelerated pressures are not without critics who worry that they may truncate the learning process by taking time and attention away from being a student (Fienberg; Hutner) and may turn graduate school into vocational school (Guillory). The pleasures of the text can wind up eclipsed by mundane matters. Nonetheless, it was once uncommon to see a job candidate with a publication or conference presentation to his or her credit. Now that much is expected—and more.

In recent years, higher education has gone through dramatic economic changes, with colleges and universities called upon to run more efficiently, and this change has, in turn, meant changes for its key personnel—faculty. English departments too have survived a period of enormously accelerated change. The field is still in the process of rethinking itself, even as it is working to reconceive its place in the evolving academy, and thus, it is necessarily having to alter its hiring practices. Whereas at one time, tenure-line faculty jobs predominated, now, increasingly, institutions are turning to contingent labor, in the form of quasi-professional instructorships with teaching loads higher than those of tenure-line faculty, or even part-time models in which freelance adjunct instructors are paid a fairly nominal amount with no health benefits. What's the problem facing graduate students, given the preponderance of these new models? It is that when you begin seeking a job, you may find only a small pool of tenure-track faculty positions for which to apply. Some of you who are committed to an academic career path may indeed choose a nontenure-line teaching position and find it sufficient—perhaps you are a creative writer working on a long novel who wants just a part-time job so that you can devote the bulk of your time and energy to writing. But others of you may instead find yourselves unhappily struggling in permanent second-class status, never secure and always striving to prove yourselves, lacking both the time and money necessary to pursue individual scholarly interests or even to keep up with the research of your chosen fields. This potential reality makes learning about nonacademic career possibilities even more critical. These paths can be very rewarding, as many former English majors will tell you, but they are by no means always linear and clear. Without the right advice, you may find yourself proceeding by trial and error through an information gathering process as you try out different possibilities.

What can you do to prepare for a career in English during such challenging times? As a graduate student coming of age professionally today, it is important for you to understand the tensions, conflicts, and challenges and to remain flexible in imagining your changing place within it all. Rather than just lamenting the scarcity of traditional tenure-track faculty positions, it is important to take action to make yourself as competitive as possible for those tenure-track opportunities that do exist. Beyond that, we also urge you to consider the field of English careers more broadly—to consider the wide range of both academic and nonacademic jobs. Teaching in a community college, for example, may not be what your faculty mentor did, but it can still be a rewarding career in its own right. Grant writing, public relations, and freelance writing though not academic paths, also have much to offer. We encourage you to take advantage of every professional development opportunity you find in your department, institution, or field.

This handbook, which is the result of years of mentoring graduate students and reflecting on our own experiences with both academic and nonacademic job searches, will also help you with your professional-development process. Our scope is necessarily limited, for we cannot hope to include all the information you need within this one book. Instead, we see our book as serving as a compendium: We provide an overview of socialization and a sampling of major issues, suggestions for important questions for you to consider, and a stock of resources for you to consult further. We encourage you not only to reach out for every relevant experience but also to read widely from the materials recommended throughout the book in order to understand the profession and its possibilities. Because we think it is vitally important for students not to fall into the "there are too few jobs" malaise, we emphasize the importance of exploring a broad range of English-related careers. We hope the book will be something you can keep close at hand and consult throughout your graduate career. Perhaps, even, it will be something your program will find useful in order to augment their professional development efforts. Whether you are an undergraduate contemplating an English graduate program and a career in the field or a beginning or advanced graduate student in an MA, MS, MFA, or PhD program in English, this guide should help you at any and every step along the way. Beginners may be most interested in the sections on how to focus an academic career in English or how to succeed as a graduate student; advanced students may find most relevant the sections on establishing oneself as a scholar, teacher, and administrator or service practitioner. Whether you are focusing on literature, rhetoric and composition, creative writing, or any of the other subfields in English studies, this guide should speak to your varied requirements by offering practical suggestions for gaining the experiences needed for long-term professional success both inside and outside academia and by providing supplementary lists of useful resources on relevant topics and issues for further exploration.

The guide is divided into six chapters:

- **Chapter 1: Determining Your Professional Goals.** This chapter invites you to consider your goals for pursuing graduate study while helping you determine the type of job that best fits your personal needs and your professional interests, as well as market realities. It also suggests you consider a broad range of possibilities for both academic and nonacademic career paths.

- **Chapter 2: Making the Most of Graduate School.** Chapter 2 demystifies many of the processes and procedures associated with graduate school, including planning course work, finding faculty mentors, and choosing thesis topics and committees, and more. It suggests you see these decisions not as arbitrary—or as a matter of graduate school only—but as a way to serve your long-range career goals.

- **Chapter 3: Establishing Yourself as a Teacher.** In this chapter, you will find advice on how to develop the kinds of teaching credentials that will be attractive to potential employers and how to present your credentials in a job application. It advises you not to stop with just the teaching experience gained through an assistantship but to reach out for alternative teaching opportunities, to make the most of the courses you are assigned, and to keep up with the "teaching conversation."

- **Chapter 4: Establishing Yourself as a Scholar.** This chapter asks you to consider the wide range of scholarly experiences that are available in a graduate-school context and how you might use these experiences to your advantage. From learning to convert seminar papers into conference papers to joining a community of scholars through publishing, you can do a lot as a student to develop scholarly credentials.

- **Chapter 5: Establishing Other Academic Selves: Service, Administration, Editing.** This chapter expands the notion of professional development to include skills developed through service, administration, and editing for both academic and nonacademic jobs. It also asks you to imagine the range of nonacademic positions that might incorporate these skills.

- **Chapter 6: Survival Strategies for Graduate School and Beyond.** Here, the guide offers practical suggestions for surviving the often-stressful conditions of advanced study. The chapter highlights the importance of developing skills in goal setting, time management, organization, and self-advocacy (among other areas)—for both immediate and long-term success.

At the end of the guide, you will find two appendixes: one that includes a selected bibliography for each chapter and another that provides helpful tips for three important aspects of the academic job-search process (application letters, teaching portfolios, and interviewing) as well as a list of useful job-search resources.

We hope that you will find this guide so useful that you will refer to it again and again throughout your graduate career—and afterward, as you continue to shape your professional persona. Most of all, we hope that it helps you achieve the results you wish—not just an intellectually rewarding graduate experience but also a satisfying and successful career in English.

Note

1. For a comprehensive discussion of these changes, see Scholes's *The Rise and Fall of English.*

References

Besimon, Estela Mara, Kelly Ward, and Karla Sanders. *The Department Chair's Role in Developing New Faculty into Teachers and Scholars.* Bolton, MA: Anker, 2000.

Boice, Robert. *Advice for New Faculty Members*. Boston: Allyn & Bacon, 2000.

Fienberg, Nina. "'The Most of It': Hiring at a Nonelite College." *Profession 1996*. New York: Modern Language Association, 1996. 73–78.

Guillory, John. "Preprofessionalism: What Graduate Students Want." *Profession 1996*. New York: Modern Language Association, 1996. 91–99.

Hutner, Gordon. "What We Talk about When We Talk about Hiring." *Profession 1994*. New York: Modern Language Association, 1994. 75–78.

Laurence, David. "The Latest Forecast." *ADE Bulletin* 131 (Spring 2002): 14–19.

Schoenfeld, A. Clay, and Robert Magnan. *Mentor in a Manual: Climbing the Academic Ladder to Tenure*. 2nd ed. Madison, WI: Magna, 1994.

Scholes, Robert E. *The Rise and Fall of English*. New Haven: Yale UP, 1998.

1 Determining Your Professional Goals

Before even applying to graduate school, it's a good idea to consider what you want from an English graduate program: Promotion at your current workplace? An academic career? Freelance writing credentials? Personal fulfillment? Then, once you have set your goals, you will want to try to find a program that will help you meet them. Of course, many people simply don't know enough about English studies or academia—or themselves—to carefully consider their long-term goals before submitting their grad-school application(s). They simply enjoy reading, writing, and discussing ideas with others, have a good sense that advanced English courses will allow them to do these things, and assume that their professional goals will become clearer to them as they work on a degree. That is, they discover what they want to do *after* graduate school when they are already *in* graduate school. If we have just described you, and you are reading this guide after already taking some courses, then you will want to consider not only what your professional goals are, but how the program you are enrolled in can help you meet your goals.

Goal 1: Licensure, Lane Change, or Pay Raise

Many people pursue graduate work because graduate courses are required for licensure (or license renewal); promotion (sometimes referred to as a "lane change"); and/or salary ("step") increases. This is especially true of public school teachers who are under increasing pressure to demonstrate their command of content areas such as English. If your goal is licensure or a change in professional status only and you plan to keep your day job, you will likely make your decision about graduate school based on convenience (i.e., the location of the school) and availability (i.e., the courses you need are offered at night, on the weekends, or during the summer). If you are a teacher, you will want to be clear with your district's Human Resources office about the courses or degree you need for the outcome you desire; you will also want to find out from the school(s) whose programs interest you whether, and when, they can offer the courses you need. It may also benefit you to find out if your school district will support your pursuit of graduate study with leave or release time or a student assistant to help with your teaching responsibilities.

Because many graduate programs have policies that limit the number of years a student can work on a degree, you will want to find out whether the degree you desire can be finished on a part-time basis, in the time frame presented. One alternative to full-time graduate work is the low-residency graduate program. Low-residency programs, which allow students to take courses on campus for a few months out of the school year and do the rest of their work by mail, are especially attractive to the growing number of master's-certified, nontenure-track college faculty who are being encouraged by their administrations to get a "terminal degree" (e.g., a PhD, DA, or MFA) or who want tenure-track jobs. One of the best known low-residency programs for composition and rhetoric specialists is offered by Indiana University of Pennsylvania (IUP). Creative writers can earn low-residency MFAs through programs offered by Vermont College and Warren Wilson College in North Carolina, among others. Other graduate programs offer a wide range of afternoon and evening classes for the convenience of students already working full time.

> One of the best known low-residency programs for composition and rhetoric specialists is offered by Indiana University of Pennsylvania (IUP). Creative writers can earn low-residency MFAs through programs offered by Vermont College and Warren Wilson College in North Carolina, among others.

Goal 2: Teaching in College

If you know that you want to teach at a college or university, you will want to first find out what kinds of positions are available, what the positions involve, and the credentials you need for the position you desire. Then, you can choose a graduate program—or tailor the program you are already in—to help you obtain those credentials. Teaching positions in academia are generally classified in three ways: (1) by the area of expertise or specialization; (2) by the teaching context [e.g., whether a school offers mostly two-year or four-year degree programs, whether the focus is on technical training or liberal-arts education, whether the school is research- or teaching-oriented] and (3) by job status and security.

Areas of Expertise

In English studies, typical areas of expertise include literature, composition and rhetoric, creative writing, technical writing, and linguistics. For hiring purposes, these areas are often divided further (e.g., early British literature, classical rhetoric, poetry writing). If you have a background in English, you have already experienced these distinctions and divisions by completing courses in different areas and then meeting specific requirements within particular subareas. You already know, for example, that literature, broadly defined, involves reading and analyzing texts, and that composition, creative writing, and tech writing involve writing texts for a variety of purposes and audiences. If you've taken a linguistics course, you know that this subarea involves looking at how language is described, used, and learned. (Rhetoric cuts across all of the other subfields by emphasizing how texts work in particular situations and why.) While there is no magic formula for determining which subarea(s) of English may be right for you, most successful academics have chosen areas that will allow them to read, discuss, and write about authors, texts, and issues that inspire or excite them—whether that be Shakespeare, the diaries of women pioneers, or how to evaluate student writing. (Again, you may already know what you enjoy, or, if you are just starting out, you may need to take some courses and talk with some professors before deciding). Additionally, it is important to at least consider job-market trends for particular subareas. (This is something that we discuss more fully below.) If, over the past few years, the number of qualified applicants in your area has far exceeded the number of advertised positions, you won't necessarily want to abandon

See *English Studies: An Introduction to the Discipline(s)* edited by Bruce McComiskey, NCTE, 2006.

your interests, but you may want to consider specializing—or, at least, gaining teaching experience—in one or two other areas of English.

Teaching Contexts

Typical teaching contexts include community and technical colleges; small liberal arts colleges; branch campuses of major research universities (often called "regional campuses"); comprehensive universities; and research universities. Historically, positions at community and technical colleges have been more teaching oriented, with faculty focusing on classroom practice and teaching four or five courses per semester, often in multiple subareas. Positions at research universities traditionally have been more research oriented, providing faculty with lighter teaching responsibilities so that they can carry out, write, and publish research—or, in the case of creative writers, create and publish poetry, fiction, and drama. Perhaps because of the scholarly expectations and the likelihood of teaching graduate seminars, faculty at research universities also tend to teach more courses in their areas of specialization. Positions at liberal arts colleges, regional campuses, and comprehensive universities have tended to require a balance between research and teaching and, in terms of teaching, attention to both general-education (e.g., introductory literature and composition) and specialized courses. Increasingly, however, community and technical colleges are encouraging faculty to present at scholarly conferences, publish scholarship, and to develop more specialized advanced courses, and research universities are putting more emphasis on good teaching at both introductory and advanced levels.

As a rule, if you want to focus on teaching a range of lower- and upper-level courses and would rather not worry too much about publishing, you will want to pursue a position outside of a research institution.

As a rule, though, if you want to focus on teaching a range of lower- and upper-level courses and would rather not worry too much about publishing, you will want to pursue a position outside of a research institution.

Status and Security

In addition to teaching context, you will need to consider whether you want to work part time or full time and if you want the security and status that comes with a tenure-track position. *Tenure track* is the term used for positions that, after a probationary period of four to six years, provide tenure, or a long-term commitment to you from the college or university. Historically speaking, tenure-track positions have been seen as more desirable than nontenure-track roles because, in addition to greater security, these positions have tended to offer better benefits, better pay, and a higher degree of status. (Tenure-track positions also typically offer opportunities to teach a greater variety of courses.) Lately, though, many universities have been moving away from tenure-track positions and toward renewable-contract positions. While in theory these positions don't offer the same security, they can in practice. That is, universities who hire faculty on fixed-term contracts often renew the contracts indefinitely, especially if the faculty members are teaching courses that are in high demand (e.g., introductory writing or literature courses) or are engaged in program administration.

Finally, you will need to consider your professional mobility. If the kind of position you desire isn't offered in your current location, will you be able to relocate? If so, how far will you be able to move? Be aware that universities typically don't hire their own graduates for tenure-track positions, as they seek diversity in experience and perspective. So, unless you will be happy teaching part time, don't expect to get a teaching job where you go to school (or even at other schools in your immediate area).

Understanding Employment Criteria

Once you know what kind of position you want, a look through one of the popular employment lists can be valuable.

For Technical and Community Colleges

According to job lists compiled by the Modern Language Association (MLA) and the *Chronicle of Higher Education*, for example, these are the common criteria for teaching at community and technical colleges:

- MA degree
- Strong commitment to teaching
- Experience teaching composition with ability to teach introductory literature and/or creative writing courses

- A willingness to advise students and serve on departmental and college committees

Many community and technical college ads also ask for a demonstrated ability to work with diverse groups of students (because these schools are often located in diverse urban areas) and technological expertise (to help support the growing number of online offerings). These same criteria often apply if you want part-time or nontenure-track work at a four-year college or university. Though ads for community-college positions typically stipulate an MA degree as the *required* qualification, it is best not to assume that an MA is the *desired* qualification. Increasingly, community colleges are hiring PhDs and ABDs ("all but dissertation") because, in a tight job market, more PhD-qualified job seekers apply to community colleges and because, in tight budget times, community colleges are competing with universities for students. If community colleges can offer courses taught by faculty with credentials similar to those at the universities, students may opt for the smaller learning context provided there. A quick look through English department rosters at community colleges will show that many faculty members have PhDs.

For Universities

For a full-time, tenure-track position at a four-year university, the criteria would most typically include:

- A PhD, considered the "terminal" or highest-level degree in English
- Specialization in a subfield (e.g., literature, composition/rhetoric, creative writing)
- Demonstrated teaching excellence (often with the ability to teach in more than one subfield)
- Conference presentations and/or journal publications in your area (or clear promise of such)
- A willingness to serve on departmental and college committees

For creative writers with a solid, or very promising, publication record, a master of fine arts (MFA) degree is often regarded as an acceptable alternative to a PhD.

Given the usual criteria for tenure-track university positions, then, you'll want to enroll in a graduate program that not only offers teaching assistantships but also allows you to teach a variety of courses. Consider, too, if the teaching-assistantship program allows you to create your own syllabi and assignments or, better yet, to design your own courses. Hiring committees are most interested in job candidates who can confidently discuss both their teaching methods and the theories and personal experiences that inform them—something that's difficult to do if you are asked to teach from a standard syllabus. Since most full-time university positions require other qualifications, keep that in mind, too. If publications are expected for these positions, you'll want a degree program that offers seminars and one-to-one faculty mentoring to help you get your writing ready for presentation and publication.

Also, look at the other experiences offered to grad students. Can you get editing experience by working on a department-sponsored journal? Administrative experience? Are there opportunities to serve on committees, so you can get service credentials? (See Chapter 5 for more on this topic.) Perhaps most important, what is the job-placement rate for the program graduates?

Specialist versus Generalist

When researching academic positions, you'll also want to consider areas of secondary expertise that are often included in ads for your area of interest. If you are primarily interested in a position teaching literature, you will note, for example, that most ads for literature faculty ask for experience teaching composition. Similarly, many ads for creative writing and composition faculty express a desire for a background in literature. Increasingly, ads for composition faculty also mention specializations such as English as a Second Language/Teachers of English to Speakers of Other Languages (ESL/TESOL), business and technical writing, computers and composition, and administration. As you look through these ads, you might decide that you would enjoy teaching many different subjects. If this is the case, you may want to prepare yourself for a "generalist" position. Generalists are prepared to teach many different kinds of courses within English—and are often interested in making connections between subfields in their teaching and scholarship. A typical ad for a generalist position would look something like that in Figure 1.1 (see page 8).

If you are interested in a position like this, you will want to choose a program that allows you to pursue many different emphases within English and, if possible, to write an "intradisciplinary" dissertation.

Assistant Professor of English to begin Fall 2005. PhD in hand by 8-15-05. Evidence of excellence in teaching first-year composition; teaching experience in at least two of the following areas of literature: classical, children's literature, modern poetry, drama. Experience teaching with technology highly desired. Faculty typically teach three courses per semester, undertake research in areas of specialization, and serve on departmental committees.

Figure 1.1. A typical ad for a generalist in English studies.

Factors Affecting the Job Search

Fluctuating Job Market

Be aware, though, that your ability to secure the position you want depends not only on the credentials you get in graduate school, but on the realities of the job market and idiosyncrasies of hiring committees. Again, as we mention in our introduction, your chances for finding a full-time, tenure-track faculty position in English right out of graduate school are about 40 percent. Sometimes, too, particular areas of the country have greater demand than others. California, New York, Florida, and Texas, for example, have many schools, so usually the opportunities are greater in those states, compared to say, South Dakota, where the population is much smaller and the number of schools fewer and farther between. Your disciplinary specialization will also affect your ability to find the job you want. For example, according to the MLA, while there were 400 jobs in composition and rhetoric advertised in the 2003–2004 Job Information List, there were just 206 in creative writing (Laurence 7).

Hidden Factors

Finally, even if your credentials, area(s) of specialization, and geographic preferences seem to match-up perfectly with an advertised position, hiring committees often have priorities that cannot be captured in position announcements—priorities that reflect their particular academic cultures. For example, faculty members at a smaller liberal-arts college may be especially interested in candidates who have a liberal-arts background and want to devote their careers to small-college teaching. Hiring committees at research institutions may be more concerned with whether a candidate's theoretical inclinations or research agenda complement those of current faculty. Graduate programs that offer mentoring sessions devoted to issues such as job-market trends and employment-search strategies provide their students with a distinct edge when it comes to negotiating these types of career concerns.

Staying Your Course

Of course, you shouldn't let market forecasts or hiring-practice lore determine your career path too much. No one can really predict the availability of positions in particular disciplinary or geographical areas or how employers will respond to applications at any given moment. (There are scores of stories about people being hired for positions that didn't even seem a good match on paper.) What we can tell you is that currently, the job market in rhetoric and composition is quite strong, literature is not so strong, and the creative writing area is very weak just now (with only 15 percent of MLA ads in 2004). So, while you want to pursue a career path that interests you, you will be wise to at least consider what you might do if, after applying for jobs, you do not find the position you really want.

Many job candidates are offered—and accept—full-time, tenure-track positions that are not ideal for them (in terms of teaching responsibilities, research expectations, geography) because they need full-time, continuing work and cannot wait around for the ideal offer to materialize. Others who desire long-term, full-time employment accept fixed-term (one- to four-year) or adjunct (part-time) positions, with the idea that they will continue to gain the teaching and/or research credentials that will eventually land them the full-time, tenure-track position they desire. As you refine your thinking, consider these questions:

- Do you need a full-time position, or will a part-time position work for you, given your career goals?
- If you require full-time work, will you be willing to accept a tenure-track position that's not your ideal?
- If you can't find the job you really want, would you be willing to consider other career options?
- If so, how will you prepare yourself to be versatile? One idea would be to consider some of the other kinds of jobs out there—both academic and nonacademic.

Goal 3: Becoming a Professional Writer or Editor

While publishing your own articles, stories, or poems can help you land (and keep) a steady, well-paid position, it often doesn't generate enough income to live on. So, if you enjoy writing—and are good at it—but you aren't interested in teaching, you may want to consider graduate work as a way to further develop your skills for a career in publishing.

Though careers in the private sector (where most professional writing and editing opportunities exist) are certainly different from those at colleges and universities, the same process for determining what credentials you will need applies. You'll want to talk with people who work in publishing and read job advertisements to get a sense of both the types of positions available and the qualifications required for them. The major academic job-opportunity lists now have categories (usually "positions outside of academe" [*Chronicle of Higher Education*, or CHE] or "nonacademic jobs" [Modern Language Association, or MLA]) that include listings for writing and editing jobs. These jobs range from freelance writing and copyediting to book-project management. One popular nonacademic source for job opportunities is *Publishers Weekly*. Their "Job Zone" can be accessed through their home page by subscribers and nonsubscribers alike. The job description for an editorial assistant, which appeared recently on the *Publishers Weekly* Web site, can be seen in Figure 1.2.

Specific duties for the position included conducting various types of research, reviewing proposals and manuscripts, proofreading final copy, securing publishing rights, and maintaining project databases and archives.

If you don't see yourself as a teacher, but you want to maintain a connection with the academic community, you should consider conduct-

---

This position assists the editor in all aspects of editing books, periodicals, and special publications. The editorial assistant works closely with the editor to be aware of all ongoing projects, allowing the department to function in the editor's absence.

Figure 1.2. An excerpt from an ad seeking an editorial assistant for a nonacademic position.

ing a focused search of job possibilities in scholarly publishing. Positions at scholarly presses can be particularly fulfilling for talented people with advanced degrees in English because they offer opportunities to not only read, evaluate, and respond to academic texts in progress but also to conduct academic research and "make serious contributions to knowledge and to shape . . . fields of study" (Demers). Scholarly presses often advertise positions in the above-mentioned job lists. Another good source for positions in this realm is the Society for Scholarly Publishing (SSP) Web site.

As is the case with teaching, there are many ways to gain the experience and expertise required for writing and editing positions while you are in graduate school. You can get some of it through your course work, for instance. It might be a good idea to look for programs that offer concentrations in many different areas of writing: nonfiction, creative, technical, professional. You will also want to carefully consider programs that support writing internships. Many schools, aware of the need for practical experience, offer internships where students volunteer their writing and editing services to an area business or nonprofit organization, for credit. Another good idea is to identify graduate programs that offer editing assistantships. Many universities, for example, sponsor literary or scholarly journals. The editors, usually also professors, often need assistance with reading and recommending manuscripts for publication, corresponding with contributors and subscribers, and editing final manuscripts for house style. There may also be opportunities within the department to help produce and edit promotional materials, department or program newsletters, or departmental web pages. Often, within English, the writing center or composition program will produce a newsletter—or maintain Web sites—and look for students who are willing to help. (See Chapter 5 for more on this topic.)

Other Avenues for English Graduates

While writing and editing positions seem a natural alternative to academic jobs, you might also consider some less-obvious career possibilities. Depending on your interests, you may find these equally fulfilling. For instance, if you like the "selling" aspect of teaching, you might enjoy working as a sales representative (rep) for a publishing company. Most of the major companies have developed long lists of books in the field of English, and such organizations are always looking

> Someone with a background in English who enjoys teaching, for example, might be interested in the announcement for an Education Specialist that the Smithsonian Institution recently posted on USAJobs, a government job site.

for good people with English backgrounds to market their products to college and university faculty. For these positions, the skills you develop as a teacher (organization, presentation, rapport with students) will be very important. Because publishing reps communicate often with their clients, you will want to make sure that you have demonstrably excellent skills in writing, too. Other possible areas for English graduates include advertising, public relations, technical writing, educational research/testing, marketing, law, and U.S. government.

If you are interested in positions like these—positions that exist outside of academia and may be only tangentially connected to English studies—you will want to spend time at your school's career-placement office, discussing with a trained professional what the options are and what qualifications are typically expected. (Some of the sources on our bibliography will help with this initial exploration.) Once you identify possible career areas, you'll then want to talk to people in those fields. What are their typical responsibilities? What skills are necessary for success? How does a person develop necessary skills? Will your graduate program offer opportunities for you to get the experience you need?

Grad School as a Means to Personal Fulfillment

Of course, many people who pursue graduate studies in English do so for personal satisfaction. They have no goal beyond reading and/or writing more and discussing ideas with others. Though they want to be challenged to improve their skills, they don't necessarily have a concrete career objective in mind. If this sounds like you, understand that it's okay to pursue a degree for personal reasons. However, you may want to assess whether taking on the demands of graduate school are worth fulfilling that personal goal.

These days, because of the competition for academic jobs, graduate schools can be very competitive places, where students feel pressured not only to perform well in courses but to present at conferences and publish. And understandably, many students who are preparing for the job market will feel pressed for time and less able to chat about ideas and books than people who are in the program for self-fulfillment. Also, faculty will tend to make themselves more available to students who are on a career track, feeling obligated to help the students get the credentials they need for a good position. The pressure increases at the MFA and PhD levels where students must, essentially, write a book manuscript. This is not to discourage you if you have more personal goals; it is meant to help you be realistic. Will the demands—and possible pressures—of graduate school be worth it to you?

It is important to note that the goals for pursuing graduate study that we've examined here are not necessarily mutually exclusive. People who enroll in graduate school may do so for multiple reasons. A public school teacher, for example, may enter a master's program to both earn a promotion and obtain credentials for an adjunct teaching position at a nearby college. Similarly, someone who starts a PhD program with personal fulfillment as a goal may discover early on that she wants to be a university professor.

Obstacles to Enrolling in Your "Dream" Program

Though many people are able to clearly define their professional goals and enroll in graduate programs that will clearly allow them to meet those goals, others are not able to do this. As we suggested at the start of this chapter, for example, many people simply don't know what they want to do until they begin doing it; through course work, an extended research project, or a teaching assistantship, a goal becomes clear. Still other potential students may have a very clear sense of their goals before applying to graduate school but, for any number of reasons, are not able to enroll in their program of choice. The program that seems the best choice for preparing a student for a career as a Medievalist at a high-powered research university, for example, may have entrance requirements (e.g., superior background in literature, foreign-language experience, excellent grades and test scores) that many applicants can't meet. Additionally, some programs are not able to offer sufficient financial support (e.g., teaching assistantships, fellowships) to everyone who meets the admission requirements. Finally, many students who want to pursue graduate studies are geographically constrained: they may qualify for a top school on the East Coast, but because they have family obligations in the Midwest, they must stay closer to home.

A similar geographic scenario involves the highly qualified student who wants to complete a graduate program in the same department in which he or she earned a bachelor's degree. Many schools make a practice of *not* accepting former students into their MA and PhD programs—especially if those students are planning academic careers. The rationale is that the best faculty members are often those who have worked with a variety of people (professors, peers, students) in many different environments.

For whatever reason, if you are a student who can't enroll in the graduate school of your dreams, don't despair. Many graduate programs exist that, while not well-endowed or prestigious, have other important things to offer, such as a vibrant local community, good faculty-student mentoring, or diverse teaching opportunities. Similarly, a school close to home may not have a program perfectly tailored to your needs, but it may be flexible enough (in terms of course work, thesis/dissertation requirements) that you can, in essence, create your own program. In the next chapters, we discuss what you can do to make almost any graduate program in English work for you.

References

Demers, Elizabeth. "Getting a Real Job in Publishing." *The Chronicle of Higher Education*. Chronicle Careers. Apr. 13, 2004. Accessed January 24, 2005 http://chronicle.com/jobs/news/2004/04/2004041301c/careers.html.

Laurence, David. "Report on the 2003–04 Job Information List." *MLA Newsletter* 36.3 (Fall 2004): 6–10.

2 Making the Most of Graduate School

Like any preprofessional experience, graduate school is often viewed as an apprenticeship—an opportunity to develop the skills you will need on the job, without many of the risks and responsibilities that come with a professional position. As you know by now, the skills you most need to develop will depend on the type of position you seek. If you're in an English graduate program—or are considering applying to one—most likely your ideal job will involve critical reading, research, writing, and/or teaching of some kind. But as we discussed in Chapter 1, some of the jobs that interest you will demand other, less-obvious abilities. Many academic positions, for example, require competencies in advising, administration, and technology. Even beyond these more concrete skills, however, most positions also require many implicit skills, such as the ability to set and attain goals, the facility to balance multiple responsibilities, the capacity to initiate and manage projects, and the finesse to supervise other employees and get along with colleagues. While these less-explicit expectations may seem so obvious as to be unnecessary to discuss, the ability to meet them often makes or breaks a career.

Of course, you will have opportunities to develop many of the most obvious skills you need in the classes you take, through departmental assistantships, and by completing a substantial scholarly project (usually a thesis or dissertation). But getting experience in areas like advising, management, and supervision—and learning to be a productive, responsible colleague—will likely require that you seek opportunities outside of the regular, published program. In this chapter, we will discuss ways that you can make the most of your graduate studies by refining your professional goals and further defining both the skills you need to meet your goals and the paths for obtaining them. Because we cover teaching, scholarship, and administration in separate chapters, we will focus only briefly on these areas here, dedicating most of this chapter to less familiar preprofessional opportunities.

Refining and Achieving Your Career Goals

Early on in her graduate program, Helen attended a professional conference, where she had the good fortune of meeting a professor in her field whose work she knew and admired. After asking Helen about her course work, the professor queried, "So, what's your five-year plan?" Helen found herself with little to say. Though she had been doing well in her courses, she hadn't thought much beyond the end of the current semester. And though she knew she wanted an academic career, she hadn't considered the particular kind of academic job she wanted or what kind of school would be the best fit for her. That professor's kind but probing questions caused Helen to think more about what she really wanted to do, where she might want to do it, and what credentials she would need.

One reason we're writing this guide is so that you won't have to wait for someone to ask you about your "five-year plan" before you start narrowing career choices, identifying relevant skills, and plotting ways to obtain them. Again, studying job ads in your chosen field, talking with professors, and consulting with people who do the kind of work you want to do is a good start. If you are not completely committed to an academic career, you will also want to talk with graduates of your program—or local businesspeople—in other fields to get a sense of the opportunities outside of academia. (Many of the books and articles included in Appendix A will also help you identify alternative career paths.) When interviewing professionals in your career area, you'll want to ask not only what their formal job responsibilities are and what types of experi-

> Many of the books and articles included in Appendix A will also help you identify alternative career paths.

ences best prepared them for those responsibilities, but you'll want to try to find out what the more tacit expectations are.

With respect to a community-college position, for example, you will want to inquire about the standard teaching requirement as well as expectations for continuing faculty development. You might ask:

- Are faculty expected to design new curricula?
- Do faculty collaborate with one other?
- Do they attend or present at conferences? If so, how are these efforts evaluated and rewarded?

If any professionals you know have been involved in hiring, you'll also want to ask what they or their colleagues look for when reviewing job applications. Consider these questions:

- Who was the last hire in your area of expertise?
- What made that person stand out from other applicants?

In gathering answers to these questions, you can begin to outline the kinds of experiences you'll need to be a competitive job candidate.

Again, if you are reading this guide before applying to graduate school, you will want to take some time to consider which program will best help you get the kind of position you want. Or, if your choices are limited for some reason (you are unable to re-locate or fear that you won't be accepted by your preferred schools), you should take some time to see if a program that doesn't seem an obvious fit might provide enough opportunities—and enough flexibility—that you can make it work for you. You'll want to think not only about the courses offered but also about other opportunities to develop professional skills. It's a good idea, too, to ask program directors about mentoring within the program:

- Does the program pair new students with experienced graduate students or faculty mentors?
- Does it offer formal opportunities to talk about career prospects in English?
- Does it support informal workshops or forums on preparing conference presentations, publishing, and/or applying for jobs?

At the same time, you want to be careful not to overdetermine your graduate-school (and career) path. While it is true that many students falter due to lack of direction, some are so firmly committed to a subfield or career goal that they fail to take advantage of opportunities that could broaden their perspectives or increase their marketability.

Recognizing the multiple professional demands placed on their graduates, many MA and PhD programs are beginning to focus more on how best to prepare students, beyond offering meaningful course work and teaching assistantships. They are starting to offer workshops and brown-bag sessions on professional-development issues, to value the time faculty devote to student mentoring, and to encourage more collaboration between faculty and students. Some programs even offer semester-long professional-development courses. If the program that interests you offers mentoring opportunities like these, consider that a plus. If you are already in such a program, take advantage of these opportunities. Find out what they are and participate in as many as possible. If the program that most appeals to you (or the one you are already in) doesn't have formal mentoring initiatives, don't despair. Just take a more active role in your own professional-development process by seeking out good informal mentoring opportunities (e.g., offering to help a professor with a project or course, joining a group of faculty and students for afternoon coffee)—or by finding ways to be your own mentor. Again, start with a list of abilities and skills you will need—from the most obvious ones to the more tacit. Then, consider how your program can help you develop them. The list of possibilities we've included here will help you begin to think about various aspects of your grad-school experience in productive ways.

The Visible Agenda: Course Work, Assistantships, Exams/Thesis/Dissertation, Faculty Advisors and Committees

Many new employees struggle in jobs because they don't understand all that's expected. As Sarah M. Dinham writes about the difficulties of being a newcomer, "Formal expectations may be expressed in the job offer, but usually they form only the most cursory hint of a complex set of varied and sometimes contradictory expectations for behavior and accomplishment" (5). Similarly, not knowing what's expected of you as a graduate student can put you at a disadvantage. Many graduate students do poorly in classes or flounder at the dissertation stage not because they are academically unprepared or unmotivated but because they simply don't know what they are supposed to do and how and when to do it. The sooner you determine what is expected of you, the better able you will be to succeed in your program and prepare yourself for the demands of your first postgraduate position.

To make sure that you have a clear sense of the more "formal" expectations for graduate school, you will need to do a little investigating. You will want to talk with graduate faculty, especially the director of graduate studies, examine a copy of the program's graduate-student handbook, and consult with current graduate students. These sources should help you determine the number of required courses and electives; the grade-point average (GPA) that must be maintained; whether (and what kind of) exams are required and how to prepare for them; and expectations for the culminating project (e.g., thesis, dissertation, or portfolio, as described below). You will also want to find out what the time frame is for completing requirements—both the average number of years it takes to finish and the outside limit. The following discussion, though necessarily general, should help you understand the kinds of questions you'll want to ask to get the information you need.

Course Work

If you know what kind of job you'll pursue after graduate school, you will want as much as possible to select courses that will help you establish the necessary background. Most graduate advisors can give you a good sense of the courses you should take for the goals you have. Some courses are required to complete any graduate program in English, no matter what your specific area of interest. Most often these include an introduction to scholarly methods and a selection of courses in the major subfields of literature; writing (e.g., composition and rhetoric, creative writing, professional writing); and linguistics. Very focused degree programs (e.g., the MFA in creative writing) will often have their own "core" requirements that reflect the particular needs of their students. Additionally, students who have been awarded teaching assistantships are often required to take a course on teaching practices and/or theories. Though program requirements may seem constraining at first—especially if you have to take courses that don't appear directly related to your research or teaching concerns—you can benefit from looking at them as opportunities to creatively explore your interests. For example, a student who knows he wants to teach English to speakers of other languages might research basic-writing pedagogy in a composition theory course and realize not only that ESL and basic writing are closely related fields but that his job prospects will improve if he establishes credentials in both areas.

Of course, tailoring course work to meet your particular needs will seem easier with electives. If you plan to teach at a community college (where faculty are generally expected to teach multiple sections of developmental and introductory composition), then you will want to try to take as many graduate-level composition and rhetoric and writing courses as you can. Literature surveys, which generally cover a variety of authors or topics, can also help prepare you to teach the introductory literature or humanities courses that many community colleges offer. If your program doesn't offer many pedagogy courses (i.e., courses that focus on how best to teach writing or literature at the college level), try to pursue projects in other courses that will help you develop your abilities to talk confidently about current teaching theories and practices. For example, finding herself in a course on modern rhetoric, a student interested in creative-writing pedagogy might survey current discussions of "writing process" to show how modern conceptions of author and text are (or are not) implied. Similarly, a literature major who wants to compile a literature-oriented teaching portfolio might approach major-area professors about the possibility of designing teaching materials, grounded in current literary scholarship, to fulfill a research requirement.

Because some programs simply can't offer all of the required—or desired—courses every semester or every year, you will want to plan your course work so that you can take all of the courses you need and want and finish within the time period you have. Talk to your graduate director about the course rotation for the next two or three years, about what's offered in the summer, and about whether faculty are open to independent studies. Independent studies (which involve a professor and student working one-to-one) can be an excellent way to gain in-depth knowledge on an issue or author and build a lasting relationship with a faculty member.

> Independent studies can be an excellent way to gain in-depth knowledge on an issue or author and build a lasting relationship with a faculty member.

Assistantship Opportunities

Most graduate programs also offer various assistantships to help their students get practical experiences beyond their course work. Among these are teaching, research, administration, and editing assistantships.

- **Teaching Assistantships.** The most common of these are teaching assistantships, which can involve tutoring (e.g., in a writing center or language-learning lab); assisting faculty with class preparation, leading discussions, and giving students feedback on their writing (more typical for MA students); or being responsible for teaching a class on your own. (See Chapter 3 for more information on teaching assistantships.) If you can imagine yourself ever teaching after graduate school, you should consider applying for an assistantship. They offer valuable experience and also financial assistance, typically through tuition remission and stipends. (Some assistantships include health benefits.) Even if you don't aspire to classroom teaching, an assistantship can help you develop the skills in organization, planning, supervision, leadership, and communication that will help you succeed in any job.

- **Research Assistantships.** In addition to teaching assistantships, many graduate programs offer research assistantships, which usually involve working with a faculty member who is conducting a major research project. Typical activities include finding source material, compiling bibliographies, checking references, interviewing research subjects, and proofreading manuscripts. This type of assistantship is especially helpful for students who enjoy research and writing and imagine themselves in a research-oriented position, whether within or outside of the academy.

- **Administrative Assistantships.** These assistantships typically involve assisting program directors with the day-to-day business of supervising departmental programs such as a general-education program, a writing center, or a composition program. Responsibilities range from planning meetings and making schedules to more substantial activities such as facilitating faculty workshops, organizing a conference, or designing a program assessment.

- **Editing Assistantships.** Finally, editing assistantships provide a chance to get hands-on experience reviewing manuscripts, making recommendations to an editor, communicating with authors, and editing work accepted for publication. They are most common in departments that sponsor academic or literary journals.

(See Chapters 4 and 5 for more specifics on research, administrative, and editing assistantships.)

Exams/Theses/Dissertations

Though completing advanced course work is a key aspect of graduate school, most programs have additional, though complementary, requirements. At both the MA/MFA and PhD levels, for example, a final exam requirement is common. Exams can be either oral or written (some programs require both) and usually occur after completion of required course work. In fact, exams are most usefully thought of as an extension of the reading, writing, and discussions that occurred in courses.

Written Exams

Typically, written exams test students' knowledge of important authors, issues, and/or movements in their major areas. Often, but not always, students design reading lists for these exams with faculty advisors who then have some control over the questions that are asked. The testing procedure usually requires students to prepare for the tests over a period of two to six months (depending upon the degree sought) and then to spend time (how much often depends again on degree sought), on campus, writing responses to the questions. Though standard practice involves onsite, supervised writing, more and more programs are allowing students to complete exams at home, in environments that are more familiar and comfortable.

Oral Exams

The content for oral exams can be similarly broad, but they often focus on a student's primary scholarly or teaching area—that which would be the basis for a thesis or dissertation. Sometimes they are an oral version of a written exam; other times, they are more of an informal discussion of research and writing plans. As the wider culture, as well as the academy that reflects it, has grown to privilege print literacy over oral literacy, oral examinations have become less common.

The Research Project

Most graduate programs in English also require a written research project of some kind. At the MA/MFA level, this project is usually called a thesis and involves researching and writing a paper of fifty to one hundred pages (sometimes more) or, in the case of creative writing students, compiling a manuscript of publishable poems, short stories, essays, or plays. Realizing that students might not always benefit from a sustained scholarly project on a single subject (or in a single genre), some schools offer alternatives to this traditional requirement. These include "starred papers" (two or three revised, usually expanded, seminar papers); a portfolio (collection of work that is either research or teaching oriented, often both); or additional course work.

At the PhD level, the culminating project is usually a dissertation. The dissertation typically requires more (or deeper) research and, thus, is frequently much longer than an MA thesis. Students are often encouraged to see it as a book manuscript or, at the least, as a collection of publishable shorter pieces (e.g., articles, essays, stories). As with exams, students usually complete these projects in consultation with faculty members knowledgeable about the scholarly area. Following submission of the culminating project, students are usually required to schedule a time to talk with faculty about the project. This conversation, often called an "oral defense," differs in formality, length, and intensity, depending on the type of degree being earned, the type of program, and, in some cases, the personalities involved. Dissertation defenses tend to be longer and more intense than MA defenses, with faculty advisors asking pointed questions about the overall approach, findings, and implications. Though sometimes intimidating, such a dialogue can often be a very good way of preparing for job-interview questions about scholarship and teaching.

As with your course work, you can make these processes go more smoothly by thinking about them early in your program and consulting with others who have successfully completed the requirements. For example, as soon as possible, try to draw connections between your career goals, course work, exams, and culminating project. What types of projects do successful hires in your field complete? How did their courses and exams prepare them for their final projects? With respect to exams, in particular, you will want not only to consult with others about process, format, and content, but also to ask for samples of successful exams. Many graduate programs maintain files of previously asked questions and passing answers to help students prepare for their own exams. In terms of the thesis or dissertation, it's a good idea to ask questions like the following:

- How long are successful projects?
- Do they typically require primary research? Secondary research? Both?
- What forms are acceptable?
- What restrictions exist concerning writing style?

Some of these questions will be answered for you in the graduate handbook distributed by your department or your school's graduate studies office. Other questions will be harder to answer because they belong to the more implicit realm of graduate-school culture. As with exams, you will want to talk with as many students and faculty as possible and review those projects regarded as particularly successful. Theses and dissertations completed by former students can usually be found in the department or school library.

Faculty Advisors

Because exams and extended scholarly projects are generally undertaken in consultation with faculty advisors, it's also a good idea to carefully consider which of your professors you would most like to work with—if you have a choice. Obviously, you will want to select faculty members who are familiar enough with your scholarly area to provide helpful feedback. Other important considerations are mutual respect and rapport. As you take your courses, consider not only which of your professors seems most knowledgeable and up to date, but which ones appear to especially appreciate your contributions to class or to offer the most encouraging responses to your writing. With which professors do you seem to have an especially good professional relationship?

It's also wise to try to find out about a professor's preferences and out-of-class personality. Consider, for example:

- Does the professor under consideration have different expectations for theses and dissertations than for course work?

- What are the professor's criteria for a finished reading list, thesis, or dissertation?

- Will the professor's responses to your work be similar to those given when you were a student in class?

- Can you determine a professor's typical turnaround time for drafts of written work? Does he or she read and respond quickly to thesis chapters, or do other commitments get in the way?

Finally, you will want to find out which professors are easy to work with outside of class. You certainly don't want to work with a professor who will accept anything (after all, you want your project to be as good as possible), but you also don't want to work with a professor who takes months to read and respond to chapter drafts or has a reputation for never approving anything. While you can ask faculty members themselves some of these questions (especially those with whom you have a good rapport), answers to other, more probing questions should be solicited from fellow students—especially those who are in the process of finishing their degree program.

> On Choosing an Advisor: With which professors do you seem to have an especially good professional relationship?

Faculty Committees

If a multifaculty committee is required (as is usually the case for final research/writing projects), you will need to determine who will be the best "director" (or key reader/responder and facilitator) and who might be best as "second readers." Once you find someone to direct the committee, he or she can help you identify and approach other possible committee members. Rapport can be a crucial factor here, too—not just between you and potential committee members but among the committee members themselves. Many a thesis or dissertation process has been delayed because of avoidable tensions between faculty members. Though you may not want to ask faculty members, point blank, if they work well together, you can tactfully raise the general issue of committee rapport with your director as you discuss potential committee members.

The Hidden Agenda: Responsibility, Collegiality, Autonomy

While graduate courses and assistantships can go a long way toward helping you develop the credentials needed for success in and beyond graduate school, most veteran professionals know that achieving success requires more than disciplinary expertise and practical experience. Much of the literature on new-faculty success, for example, suggests that those who do well during their first years on the job are able to meet both the formal, explicit expectations that others have for them, as well as the unstated expectations, such as self-initiative and collegiality. Indeed, these invisible or tacit expectations can not only make or break a career, but they can determine your fate as a graduate student. Many students who exceed in the most obvious aspects of career development (for example, those who attain stellar grades or earn competitive fellowships), are unable to find fulfilling jobs because they have not focused enough on developing the people skills that employers value. These same students, though bright and enthusiastic, may inadvertently offend professors and peers, which can result in a rough ride through graduate school. As with more formal expectations, it can help to talk with your graduate director and faculty about the hidden values and mores of your department and program. In many cases, though, your peers—especially those who have spent time in the program—can offer the most valuable insights.

Responsibility

In these times of budget cuts and thinning resources, employers are especially interested in hiring people they can count on to work harder, do better, and meet tougher deadlines than their predecessors—often under less-than-ideal circumstances (e.g., without extra pay or sufficient guidance). In some areas, including many academic fields, jobs are so scarce and applicants so plentiful that hiring teams have no choice but to look beyond obvious qualifications (good grades, relevant course work, related experience) to more elusive qualities that set candidates apart. One such quality is responsibility, which, in typical workplace settings, involves the ability to both understand and meet (or, more likely, exceed) professional expectations.

Graduate school, with its many and varied requirements, offers numerous opportunities to demonstrate, or further develop, the ability to reach the goals that future supervisors will set for you. Of course, most people who pursue graduate studies want to do well and have every intention of meeting the expectations of their professors, program directors, and/or department chairs. The problem is that many of these expectations are unwritten and/or unspoken; by virtue of being in graduate school, you are just supposed to know them. For example, many new graduate students don't realize that professors usually have much higher expectations for reading and writing at the graduate level than for the undergrad (even senior) level. Reading assignments are heavy (three hundred pages per week, per course, is not uncommon), and the texts themselves are often highly theoretical and require much time and thought. In terms of written work, new students are often unprepared for the emphasis on original research, in-depth analysis, and fluid, flawless writing. These heightened expectations can be especially difficult for graduate students who received their undergraduate degree from the same department and have some of the same professors. Suddenly, where summary of an argument may have fulfilled a writing requirement in the spring, in the fall, it is subpar.

New graduate students often also aren't aware that graduate faculty expect perfect attendance (i.e., no absences from class); thorough class preparation (i.e., all assigned work has been completed); regular and high-quality class participation; and close attention to deadlines. While professors are often more flexible with requirements and policies at the undergrad level—especially with students who aren't English majors— their practices change at the graduate level because the purpose of the courses change. Graduate courses are intended not only to provide students with background knowledge, but to prepare them to be successful professionals. Professionals are on time, prepared, and ready to submit quality work. Though most faculty are happy to help students negotiate the high expectations of graduate school and prepare for a competitive job market, they most respect those who are self-motivated and self-sufficient—the ones who hear a vague reference to a critic in class, for example, and take the time to look it up in a database and apply it to that week's topic.

Collegiality

"Good Citizen" Skills

Most employers, whether academic or not, are looking not only for able, creative, energetic employees but also for people with whom they can easily imagine working. If you consider that most of us spend half of each day on the job, then it's easy to see why collegiality, or the ability to get along with others, is incredibly important. At the most basic level, you will need to recognize what it means to be a good colleague. Good colleagues are approachable, respectful, and fair. If they don't like someone else in their office, department, or program, they try, as much as possible, to keep it to themselves. Good colleagues volunteer help when it is needed—and don't expect favors in return. They encourage and celebrate the good work of others, even when their goodwill gestures seem to minimize their own accomplishments.

As with responsibility, you can take advantage of graduate school to develop the kind of "good citizen" skills that will serve you well in your graduate program and beyond. Most academic settings, like their private-sector equivalents, require a good deal of social interaction—not only between faculty and students but among faculty, who are required to serve on committees together, plan curricula together, and coauthor

proposals and reports. Knowing that students will be asked to collaborate after graduation, many programs and professors build in opportunities to work with others—through collaborative projects in courses,
peer-mentoring programs, and team-teaching opportunities. For
example, it is very common for graduate directors or teaching-assistant
supervisors to ask veteran graduate students to visit required graduate
classes or new-teaching assistants' (TA) meetings to help orient new
students. Similarly, professors often invite graduate students at the thesis
or dissertation stage to visit courses and speak about their research
interests and findings. If occasions such as these arise in your program,
take advantage of them as much as possible.

　　If your program doesn't include such built-in opportunities, find
other, informal ways to build good relationships with faculty and peers.
Organize a study group for an upcoming exam and bring the refresh-
ments. Host an end-of-term party to help celebrate student accomplishments (including your own). Offer to bring your collection of Picasso
prints to class when your professor is lecturing on Gertrude Stein. Not
only will these contributions give you an edge in the job-application
process (because your professors and peers will remember them and
note them in reference letters or in conversations with hiring-committee
members); they will help you survive graduate school. Because advanced study can be an isolating, nerve-wracking process, you will want
to build as many bridges and make as many friends as possible. (We talk
more about this in our last chapter.) You will need all the smiles and
support you can get!

Productive Working Relationships

In addition to honing your relationship-building skills, graduate school
offers many opportunities to nurture abilities needed to *maintain*
productive working relationships. As is true of any social scene, academic departments and programs are political spaces, shaped by
differing disciplinary interests and worldviews. Often, the politics are
generative; the differences are seen as helpful, even necessary. Sometimes, though, these differences lead to unbridgeable professional
disagreements and, in the worst of cases, personal animosities. As a
student, you will probably hear about tensions between faculty members secondhand, through the student grapevine. Don't be surprised,
though, if a professor (or two) expresses displeasure with a colleague in
front of you—especially if that professor is your advisor and you are
fairly advanced in your degree program. Though professors know they

should not engage students in office politics, sometimes the feelings become too intense to contain. In either case, whether the gossip arrives first- or secondhand, you should resist the temptation to participate in it. As one reviewer of our book wisely pointed out, "Much better to be thought of as a person with poise and discretion, rather than 'the' person who several semesters or years ago said this or that about someone else."

Autonomy

Though the ability to work with others is an important, highly-valued aptitude, the literature on faculty success also suggests that self-reliance, or "autonomy," is crucial. Faculty who succeed (like their nonacademic counterparts) are able to set and meet goals, make decisions on their own about key aspects of their careers, and initiate projects and pro-grams. As Walker and Hale write, such faculty "feel in control." "They do not feel restricted by the choices of others nor by the shortcomings of the environments in which they work" (220). This doesn't mean that you will be expected to fend for yourself but, rather, that you should not seem overly dependent on others. Unfortunately, because graduate school can feel especially hierarchical (i.e., professors seem to have all the power—over fellowships, grades, job offers, etc.), students tend to depend a little too much on faculty advice and encouragement. Such dependence can put you at a disadvantage if, as a new hire, you are asked right away for your opinions on important matters, to design a course, or propose revisions to curricula.

So, as much as you can, try to set your own agenda in graduate school (again, based on your career objectives) and stick to it. If your goal is teaching full time at a university, do all you can to not only teach a variety of courses but to create interesting versions of those courses. (We'll talk more about this in Chapter 3.) If you know you'll be required, long term, to maintain an active research agenda, get started right away by organizing conference panels and submitting abstracts. (We talk more about this in Chapter 4.) In short, don't wait for others to involve you in career-building projects or to convince you of your abilities. If you do, you may find yourself in the final stages of your degree program with little to show a prospective employer who wants to know why he or she should hire you.

Of course, despite expectations of autonomy in graduate school and beyond, many faculty members (and employers) will assume that the program agenda and career path that worked for them will work for you, too. Professors who landed their dream job at a research-oriented university and successfully published their way through tenure and promotion are sometimes surprised when their students express a desire to work at a community college. Similarly, those who moved long distances to follow their career goals are often befuddled by students who want to find a position close to home, even if it means lower status and pay or less security.

It's important to remember that you—not your professor—will have to live with your choices. Besides, there's no guarantee that the type of position your professor sought will even be available when you are ready to send out applications. In research conducted for a recent report of the MLA Committee on Professional Employment, Cheryl Glenn found that in the United States, "over 90% of English programs and most likely between one-half and two-thirds of the total number of professorial-rank appointments are located outside doctorate-granting institutions." "Given these percentages," Glenn asserted, "the message seems clear: the primary goal of graduate education should not be to replicate the graduate faculty" (MLA Committee).

Expectations Regarding Theory

Aside from longer, more complex reading and writing assignments, most graduate professors will expect you to develop an understanding of current theories in the field (e.g., theories about how language works, how readers interpret texts, how writing is best taught). Theoretical knowledge is important because it can help you appreciate the reasons why academics might interpret the same text differently or teach the same skill in different ways. It can also help you understand your own reading, writing, thinking, and learning processes. Because entire books are devoted to differentiating and discussing theoretical perspectives common to work in English (some of these books are included in our first appendix), we will limit our treatment here to some general recommendations for thinking about theory as a student.

First, it is helpful to recognize that theoretical perspectives reflect, to a sometimes large degree, how academics view themselves, the world, and the connection between themselves and others. In fact, scholars who interpret the same literary work differently may see core concepts like "truth" or "ethics" in different ways. This is why seemingly benign disagreements about how something should be read or taught can turn into heated political debates that affect people in very personal ways. It is also why graduate students often find themselves being persuaded by faculty and fellow students to join one theoretical camp or the other. Our best advice to students beginning to learn theory is to read a good introduction to current theoretical perspectives (e.g., Eagleton's *Literary Theory* or Tate, Rupiper, and Schick's *A Guide to Composition Pedagogies*) that highlights the differences between perspectives and the reasons for the differences—and then read some of the key primary texts (or excerpts from these texts) that more fully articulate the theory. (Because some of the primary texts are very difficult to read, it's best if you can read them in a course, with the guidance of a professor.) Though you will surely feel more affinity for some theories than others, you will benefit greatly—as a scholar, a writer, and a teacher—by carefully considering not only what each theory means, but how it contributes (or has contributed) to the field. What does this theory offer that others don't? What issues does it highlight? What questions can it help answer? What questions does it seem to ignore? In what ways is it similar to/ different from other theories? By using this process of reading and questioning, you will develop a clear understanding of both the theories themselves and the people who employ them. Most importantly, you will prepare yourself to make a conscious choice about what theory (or, more likely, theories) you will use for your own scholarship and teaching.

> Our best advice to students beginning to learn theory is to read a good introduction to current theoretical perspectives and then read some of the key primary texts (or excerpts from these texts) that more fully articulate the theory. Because some primary texts are very difficult to read, it's best if you can read them in a course, with the guidance of a professor.

Looking Ahead to the Job Search

As we have stressed throughout this chapter, you can actually start preparing for your job search from the time you walk into your first graduate class—especially if you know what kind of position you want and the credentials needed to be a strong applicant.

- If you know early on, for example, that your dream job will require research and publication, imagine how you might channel work you are already doing toward that goal.
  - Consider how a seminar paper might be the first stage in a larger scholarly project (instead of just a course requirement).

- Is there a topic or issue that you could begin researching in an introductory survey course and continue to explore in subsequent specialized courses?

- Is the topic one that would work well for a presentation at a local conference or publication in a regional journal? (More on this in Chapter 4.)

■ If you can imagine yourself in an administrative position, find out what you might do now or in the near future to develop this aspect of your professional life.

- Does your program offer administrative assistantships? If so, how are they awarded?

- What can you do to make yourself a viable candidate for such an assistantship?

- If there are no administrative assistantships, can you volunteer your time and talents to assist your graduate coordinator? Writing program director? Director of undergrad studies? (Read more on this in Chapter 5.)

> Even if you are undecided about your specific career goals, you can anticipate the professional qualities that any employer would desire and take advantage of opportunities to develop and demonstrate them.

Even if you are undecided about your specific career goals, you can anticipate the professional qualities that any employer would desire (e.g., creativity, initiative, excellent communication skills, collegiality) and take advantage of opportunities to develop and demonstrate them.

Learning about the Search Process

Another good way to prepare for a successful job search is to find out how the search process actually works. If your program offers brown-bag sessions on how to apply for relevant positions, attend them—even if you won't be "on the market" for a couple of years. It's good to know in advance the typical contents of a strong résumé or vita and to imagine how you will communicate your own experiences and expertise to potential employers through cover letters and interviews. It's also useful to find out early about other materials that employers typically expect from applicants. If your program doesn't offer formal professional-development opportunities, then you will want to take it upon yourself to get examples of application materials, write preliminary drafts, and share your drafts with as many people as possible—especially people who have helped hire for the types of positions you are interested in. (Take a look at the writing tips and various guides in Appendix B for more specific information on the academic job search.)

The Importance of Good References

Because, in addition to the application materials mentioned above, most employers ask for references, you will want to develop the kinds of relationships with professors and supervisors that will allow them to discuss your abilities and potential with confidence. And, because a weak reference is actually worse than no reference at all, confirm with all potential recommenders that they will be able to talk about you with enough detail and enthusiasm to help you get the job you want. If you know that recommendation letters will be required (some employers prefer to call references), ask for these letters early (preferably, two months before applications are due), so your references will have plenty of time to write thorough letters. It's also a good idea to remind recommenders about the various facets of your relationship with them (e.g., courses you took with them, grades you earned, projects you completed), so they can support general claims about your excellent qualities with specific examples.

Now that you have a general idea about what you can do, as a student, to succeed in graduate school and prepare yourself for a potentially tight job market, you are ready to think more specifically about how to develop your skills in the areas that are most likely to be stressed in advertisements for positions in the field of English. Our next three chapters—on teaching, scholarship, and administration/service/editing, respectively—will give you a good start.

References

Dinham, Sarah M. "Being a Newcomer." *Faculty in New Jobs: A Guide to Settling In, Becoming Established, and Building Institutional Support.* Ed. Robert J. Menges and Associates. San Francisco: Jossey-Bass, 1999.

Eagleton, Terry. *Literary Theory: An Introduction.* 2nd ed. Minneapolis: U of Minnesota P, 1996.

MLA Committee on Professional Employment. "Final Report." 7 April 1998. Updated 11 July 2003. Accessed 25 July 2005 < www.mla.org/resources/documents/rep_employment/prof_employment >.

Tate, Gary, Amy Rupiper, and Kurt Schick. *A Guide to Composition Pedagogies*. New York: Oxford UP, 2001.

Walker, Charles J., and Natalie M. Hale. "Faculty Well-Being and Vitality." *Faculty in New Jobs: A Guide to Settling In, Becoming Established, and Building Institutional Support*. Ed. Robert J. Menges and Associates. San Francisco: Jossey-Bass, 1999. 216–39.

3 Establishing Yourself as a Teacher

T eaching is one of the most rewarding and significant aspects of academic life and an important part of what is learned in an English graduate program. Most of us have vivid recollections of those special teachers along the way who touched us deeply and changed our way of thinking, if not our lives. The prospect of becoming one of those people to someone else is a big part of what pulls us to graduate school.

However, once you are there, it is important to develop the kinds of teaching credentials that will be attractive to potential employers. After all, experience counts much more than simply suggesting potential, as it does for any prospective job. Therefore, it is important to obtain as much of a teaching background as possible—provided, that is, that you are not so overloaded that it interferes with your scholarly work. In addition to helping you secure that all-important first job, extensive teaching experience, if you are planning an academic career, means that you won't have to spend an inordinate amount of time as an assistant professor (or other first position) learning how to teach. Simply put, if you have to spend too much time at that point learning to teach, you will have less time for other professional demands, such as publishing, administrative work, and service. If you are planning on applying your teaching experience toward a nonacademic job, perhaps by training employees or running employee groups, then the more experience you have coping with all the challenging aspects of teaching, the more quickly you can adapt to other aspects of your new work context. This chapter invites you to

- Review your long-term career goals to determine the kinds of teaching experiences you will likely need
- Consider common ways to gain and make the most of these experiences
- Figure out how to keep up with the ever-changing "teaching conversation"
- Gain scholarly credentials inside and outside English that will broaden your range of teaching expertise
- Demonstrate your credentials when you go on the job market

Review Your Long-Term Career Goals

In what sort of position do you see yourself five, ten, or even twenty years down the line? As we discussed in Chapter 1, traditional research and teaching institutions offer very different kinds of careers. Yet, these institutions do not really represent a binary, so much as they do a continuum of teaching possibilities. Imagine a continuum ranging from a selective research institution in which faculty may teach only two to four graduate seminars a year with the rest of their time devoted to scholarship to a typical community college in which faculty may teach twelve or more courses per year with little or no research expected. In between are a variety of mid-range institutions in which scholarship and teaching responsibilities may be more balanced.

Identify Your Preferences

So, one place to start envisioning your future is to think about what mix of teaching and research, and, in some cases, administration, you would ideally like to have. Then consider what you could also be happy doing, given a potentially tight market in your field; your own preferences or restrictions, such as accommodating a spouse's career or needing a particular geographic location; and your own professional strengths and weaknesses. Keep in mind that your professors and mentors may have different values and expectations than you yourself may have. If they joined a demanding research university with a PhD program, they may encourage you to go down the same path. That may or may not be possible for you—either because you prefer teaching to research, or simply because there are a limited number of research-oriented jobs in your discipline. Or, if you would prefer a non-academic career, what kind of teaching might you do and how much of your work time do you wish to spend on it?

> Keep in mind that your professors and mentors may have different values and expectations than you yourself may have.

Here are some questions for you to consider as your review your goals:

- Do you enjoy doing research, and would you prefer to devote most of your time to it rather than to teaching? Or do you find your heart is really more in the classroom than in the library?

- Do you ideally imagine yourself teaching primarily graduate courses, perhaps in a specialized area such as Renaissance literature or history of rhetoric? These career paths are found primarily in PhD-granting departments at research universities.

- Would you like to teach a variety of graduate and undergraduate courses, perhaps including your area of expertise, but also extending beyond that into a variety of other areas? These career paths are found primarily in MA-granting departments in universities.

- Would you like to teach a more generalized variety of under-graduate courses (composition, literature, creative writing)? These career paths are found primarily in BA-granting depart-ments at teaching universities, small schools, and community colleges.

- Would you like to teach not only literature or composition or creative writing but also teach beyond English studies in pro-grams such as women's studies, black studies, or English as a second language? These career possibilities can be found at many kinds of schools.

- Would you like to mix teaching with not only research but also administration? Perhaps you would enjoy running a writing program or directing a graduate or undergraduate program, or eventually chairing a department. These career paths can be found at nearly every kind of school.

- If you are planning a career outside academe, to what sorts of teaching-related activities might you apply your graduate teaching experience? Perhaps you will be training employees, running workshops, or leading discussions. How much time, ideally, do you wish to devote to these teaching activities? Does your desired job also require research and administration, and, if so, what kinds? How much?

Identifying your preferences can help you choose a direction in which to focus your teaching choices. However, you may also want to prepare for more than one teaching scenario. Those academic positions emphasizing research, for example, are fewer and therefore more competitive. So, even if research is your preference, you may find yourself applying for and accepting a different kind of job.

Consider a Range of Career Possibilities

It is wise to apply for a broad range of career possibilities; that way, you can perhaps choose one that comes close to meeting your needs. Some former job seekers will testify that even though the position they eventually were offered was not what they originally envisioned, they are very happy with the balance of teaching and research they got. Some people who would have preferred a career emphasizing research but wound up taking a position stressing teaching, try to publish as much as possible and keep an eye on advertisements for positions more to their liking. However, this strategy may not work if the teaching load is so heavy that it precludes much scholarly publishing. Others find ways to conduct research anyway, though in smaller amounts than they might prefer, for example, by applying for grants that release them from part of their course load. Or they may find that doing administration, or a combination of administration and teaching, frees up some time for research. Still others simply reevaluate their attitudes toward teaching and conclude that it is more rewarding than they may have originally thought, particularly once they can teach a wide variety of courses. So, while in graduate school, try to be flexible as you consider the broad range of academic career possibilities.

Ways to Get Teaching Experience in Graduate School

Graduate schools typically offer a variety of teaching experiences. In all these configurations for teaching, the amount of responsibility and visibility you carry can be small (serving as an anonymous grader for a large course) or large (independently designing and teaching your own course). All of them, however, are valuable ways to get different perspectives on teaching. A rule of thumb for making teaching choices in graduate school is simply to reach out for as much experience as possible. Following are some typical opportunities that you may encounter.

> A rule of thumb for making teaching choices in graduate school is simply to reach out for as much experience as possible.

Classroom Teaching

Many graduate programs offer a variety of opportunities for graduate students to assist in a course that a faculty member is actually teaching, often with this assistant role serving as a precursor to later teaching their own courses. In one common arrangement, for example, your role might be simply to respond to student writing or even to grade work. Large introductory literature classes are often run this way. This kind of assistant position enables a department to have a large cost-saving enrollment for a given course, since the assistant's help in responding to writing saves the faculty member so much time. It enables graduate students to gain experience in how to respond to writing effectively and efficiently and to observe the teaching of the faculty member at close range. In other teaching arrangements, you may assist faculty both inside and outside English in relatively small courses often called "writing intensive" or "writing enriched." These courses sprang up years ago when the writing across the curriculum movement asserted that students need attention to writing in courses beyond the traditional ones provided by English departments. Today, you may be called upon to assist in courses in fields as diverse as physics, history, or engineering. Your responsibilities for teaching writing are greater than those for grading assistantships, as you may initiate a variety of activities, including responding to multiple drafts, collaborating in designing an assignment with appropriate writing criteria, and perhaps leading short class sessions on particular writing issues or working with students one-to-one outside class. And these are just two common examples of a variety of possibilities for assisting faculty in classroom settings; there are many more.

> Typically, programs provide training in how to teach, including preservice workshops and ongoing support on a variety of pedagogical issues.

Many graduate programs also permit graduate students to teach their own courses. At some schools, new graduate students are placed immediately into their own courses, while at others, they may first assist a faculty member in a course or tutor in a writing center before taking on their own classes. Typically, programs provide training in how to teach, including preservice workshops and ongoing support on a variety of pedagogical issues such as how to construct a syllabus, develop assignments, and respond to student writing. Traditionally, graduate students start out with first-year writing courses and then go on to teach any number of courses in composition, literature, or creative writing. However, individual programs vary. So, in some places, for example, graduate students are allowed to teach only first-year writing, while in others they may immediately begin teaching other courses. In composition, a graduate student may take on basic writing, advanced writing, and specialty courses such as argumentation and writing in the disci-plines. In literature, students may assist a faculty member in teaching a course, thereby receiving one-to-one mentoring, or they may join several other graduate students and a faculty member in teaching a large introductory literature class with breakout sections assigned to each instruc-tor. At a later time, instructors may then be assigned their own specialty literature courses. Other programs may simply put graduate students immediately into their own literature courses. In creative writing, teaching assistants may teach an introductory course in such areas as fiction or poetry, perhaps after assisting with a faculty member's course first.

> Individual programs vary. So, in some places, for example, graduate students are allowed to teach only first-year writing, while in others they may immediately begin teaching other courses.

Tutoring in Writing

Tutoring can also be a valuable way to learn how to respond to writing effectively and efficiently. You might tutor in one-to-one individualized sessions in a writing center, or serve as a tutor for a large course or department. In a typical tutoring session, you will have only a half hour at most to help students with a variety of writing and reading problems, ranging from trying to understand an assignment, to finding a topic, to organizing/reorganizing a piece, to editing and proofreading for clarity. Tutoring gives you a close-up view of students that you often cannot get when teaching twenty or more students at once. You see what works and what doesn't work at specific points in writing, along with the sorts of difficulties students have in deciphering faculty assignments. You also learn about the special challenges of a diverse range of students including nonnative speakers, first generation college students, and students with disabilities, for example. With tutoring, as with assisting in writing-intensive courses, you learn about how different the demands and conventions of writing are in different disciplines.

> Tutoring can be a valuable way to learn how to respond to writing effectively and efficiently.

Teaching with Technology

As technology has transformed the way we deliver services in the classroom and the writing center, a variety of opportunities for gaining teaching experience have opened up. For example, you may

- Teach a course completely online, never meeting in a classroom
- Collaborate and assist a faculty member in some way in online teaching, perhaps by responding to writing on your own or with several other teaching assistants
- Hold online tutorial sessions for a writing center

Technology can also be used to enhance a regular course if you put your syllabus and supporting materials online on its own Web site. This site may contain course readings, instructions for formal and informal writing, discussion listservs and bulletin boards, reference materials, and other information. These possibilities are found primarily in English departments or extension programs.

Time spent exploring technical possibilities is worthwhile, as this kind of experience is greatly in demand on the job market. Typically, graduate students either take a special course or workshop in order to acquire the necessary technical skills to teach or tutor online, or these skills are folded into a department's general teacher training program. From this experience, you learn about the many ways in which technology can enhance or substitute for an actual classroom or tutoring center.

Teaching outside the Academy

The kinds of teaching done across the field of English studies also occur in a variety of settings outside English departments that you can seek out for yourself. Here are a few brief examples, just to give you a sense of the varied possibilities:

- **Prison Literacy Efforts.** Prisons often offer formal or informal education programs for their inmates. You might teach a traditional course in writing, literature, or creative writing, or you could design your own course.

- **Nursing Homes.** Nursing homes are only one of many kinds of outreach to the elderly, including, for example, organizations that sponsor travel, short field trips, workshops, and courses. You could propose any number of courses, such as journal writing or techniques for writing poetry.

- **Community Education.** Your city or town may offer a variety of English-related courses such as regional literature, journal writing, grammar, beginning poetry, and others, for a minimal fee. Such courses might be held in the local high school, the public library, or a community center. Here, too, technology has transformed the face of community learning, with the "community" you reach virtually limitless. An informal course on the Nancy Drew mysteries or a formal course on essay writing could reach community groups across your state or even the nation.

These are just a few examples, but the number of settings for learning outside the academy is constantly expanding. By seeking out these possibilities, you can expand your repertoire of teaching experiences to include a variety of topics and students—and to see the difference it makes teaching without having to assign grades.

Making the Most of Your Teaching Assignments

Graduate programs that train teachers differ in a variety of ways:

- In the philosophical and theoretical approaches they emphasize
- In the amount of freedom and guidance they provide
- In the kinds of teaching opportunities they offer

In many cases, you may simply have to attend whatever program accepts you. But if you are in a position to choose, try to find out as much as you can about your prospective training situation. Consider questions such as these:

- Do they offer a "preservice" training workshop?
- Is there ongoing training?

- What is the theoretical approach or approaches to teaching advocated by the program? What kinds of courses will you be able to teach?
- What balance of freedom and structure do individual instructors have?
  - Do they teach from a common syllabus or work from common samples?
  - Do they teach from a common text, choose from a small selection of books, or choose any text?
- What pedagogical practices does the program advocate?

Ideally, select a program that offers guidance and structure but still allows you enough freedom to discover yourself as a teacher. If you are already teaching for a graduate program, make the most of whatever it offers and try to go beyond it, if you can, to get ample teaching experience and expertise. Here are some examples of things to do while in graduate school, in order to position yourself well for your chosen career path:

Identify Your Teaching Philosophy

A teaching philosophy is the set of values and beliefs that informs your choices in the classroom. Your philosophy gets at why you do what you do; it gives your varied teaching practices some intellectual coherence. Typically, you develop a teaching philosophy either over time as a result of exposure to ideas in your program, teaching practicum, and course work or through your mentoring experiences with faculty, discussions with graduate student colleagues, or, perhaps, most of all, through the trial-and-error practices of your own teaching.

Since there are so many approaches to teaching literature, composition, and creative writing, you must identify those that best fit your outlook, while being aware that some approaches are more current than others in your English subdiscipline. See which approaches best reflect your inclinations and use them to describe your classroom goals and how you reach them.

In the Literature Classroom

- What is your overriding goal for the students? Why?
- Will you mostly lecture, hold discussions, or do both?
- What sorts of papers will you have students write—analyses, personal responses, or creative responses?

In the Composition Classroom

- What are your goals for the students? Why?
- Will you use writing groups, portfolios, and teach aspects of the writing process?
- What sorts of papers will students write—academic essays, personal narratives, or hybrid papers?
- Will you use a reader, and, if so, what kind?

In the Creative Writing Classroom

- What are your goals for the students? Why?
- Will you teach special techniques, use writing groups, or assign exemplary readings? What kinds of creative pieces will students write?

If, for these and other choices, you get into the habit of asking yourself *why* you are doing what you are doing—and *how* various activities and assignments work together—you will develop the intellectual coherence of a teaching philosophy.

Eventually, when you interview for a teaching position, your prospective employers will likely ask that you explain your philosophy, so that they can determine whether your approach will fit with theirs. Be aware that not only individual teachers but also programs themselves differ in their teaching philosophies. When conducting research for your interview, then, you will want to identify the teaching philosophy that best describes that program: What textbooks do they use? What do any samples of syllabi you collect suggest about their classroom practices? Is their philosophy stated explicitly in their mission statement? Once you determine a program's philosophy, you will want to think carefully about how your own preferred approaches coincide or differ. Some programs will fit you better than others, so you may find that you need to either look elsewhere, or adjust components of your philosophy to match theirs.

Experiment with All Aspects of Teaching

Graduate programs may vary enormously in the amount of freedom individual instructors have over the content of their assigned courses in composition, literature, and creative writing. For example, some schools prefer instructors to work with a common textbook and syllabus, while others allow instructors to choose their own texts and determine their own course content. Even if you find yourself in a more-restrictive program, you can still find ways to develop individually. After all, though most graduate programs offer valuable guidelines, no one recipe works flawlessly for every instructor, so plan to experiment. Try even subtle variations—an extra ten-minute class activity, a particular kind of writing comment—and then get feedback from students to see how it worked. The more you experiment and assess, the faster you will build confidence and expertise in your teaching.

Keep an Informal Teaching Log

Some graduate programs require students to keep a reflective log or journal. If your program has no such requirement, begin keeping a log for your own purposes. After each class you teach, take a few minutes to reflect on it in your log. Through writing, you may discover a variety of issues, questions, or memorable teaching moments that will ultimately help you not only improve your teaching but also get to know yourself as a teacher.

Ask Your Students for Feedback

Programs typically have standard surveys for instructors to distribute at the end of a course that invite student commentary on both the course and the teaching. It can be very helpful to review survey results closely, looking for any patterns that may appear over time. Once you've gathered at least three sets of surveys, you may notice that your scores on a particular item—explaining assignments well, for example—are consistently lower than those for other items. Seeing this pattern can then prompt you to review your assignments, consult other teachers, and read books or articles about assignment writing for ideas to improve in that area. You can follow up by checking that item on subsequent surveys to see if your score improves. Beyond reviewing the standard surveys, however, you can also devise other useful forms of feedback such as the following:

- **Your Own End-of-Course Surveys.** Surveys you design yourself can help you gather even more specific feedback. You can ask, for instance,

  - what assignments were most instructive

  - what readings seemed most interesting

  - what students learned from the course

- what students suggest you change the next time you teach it.

- **Midcourse Evaluations.** Generally, by midterm, students have settled in to your course and are able to offer constructive feedback. You might

  - devise a survey for students to take anonymously

  - meet with students individually both to give them feedback on their performance thus far and to get any comments from them

  - take class time to have a discussion about how the class is working out.

- **Unit Surveys.** Perhaps your class is structured by lesson plan or unit. When work is turned in, you can ask students to reflect on the unit and what activities helped them learn.

- **Ongoing Feedback.** Build in-class time for students to reflect on any activity you devise. After a set of readings or class activities, stop to ask them what they learned and whether it made sense. This sort of ongoing feedback informs you immediately and can save you from a situation that happens to nearly all teachers at least once: moving along for several classes before discovering that a key piece in the class sequence never really made sense to your students.

> Closely review the results from student surveys given at the end of each course, looking for any patterns that may appear over time. . . . Seeing a pattern of low marks in regard to any particular practice can prompt you to review your assignments, consult other teachers, and read books or articles . . . for ideas to improve in that area.

Observe Other Teachers; Invite Others to Observe You

If your program doesn't offer classroom observation opportunities, set up your own. Invite peers to sit in on your class and ask to sit in on theirs. What you learn from both experiences can prove to be extremely helpful.

- **Observers in Your Classroom.** Observers may comment on any number of issues—the flow of your class, whether your voice can be easily heard, and which students are engaged or disengaged.

This sort of attentive observation can point to issues that are hard to see when you are busy actually teaching or those you may miss in your own reflections.

- **Observing Others.** By observing peer classes, too, you can see firsthand what a similar class looks like from another perspective, or you can observe teaching styles that may be quite similar to or radically different from yours. The main rule of thumb for an accurate observation is to play "junior anthropologist"—seeing as much as you can and writing it down, observing but avoiding harsh judgment. One way to accomplish this kind of observation is to meet with your observer ahead of time to describe your goals, plans, and concerns—either for the class to be observed or perhaps for your teaching overall. You can then ask for specific feedback on these issues.

> Attentive observation can point to issues that are hard to see when you are busy actually teaching or those you may miss in your own reflections.

- **Benefits of Both Experiences.** Though peer observation exchanges yield useful information, you may also wish to have a faculty mentor, or perhaps director of the program, observe your class if your program hasn't arranged that. The observations of these experienced teachers can be particularly helpful, especially if they offer strategies for solving problems.

Keeping Up with the Teaching Conversation

Teaching in English studies is by no means a static or finite enterprise, something to be learned and then set aside when you move on to something else. Instead, it is a dynamic and ever-changing professional conversation of which you need to stay abreast. New methods, new ideas, and new approaches are constantly appearing and evolving. Figure 3.1 offers some brief examples just to give you a sense of the kinds of topics under discussion. Keep in mind that there are many more.

The topics listed in Figure 3.1 only scratch the surface of recent conversations about teaching. Where can you learn more about teaching-related discussions in your area of interest?

Teaching with Technology: Technology has transformed teaching in many ways over the last decade, enabling teachers to create sites of electronic discussion to complement traditional discussions; allowing students to draft, transmit, and revise drafts electronically; and even making it possible for classes to be offered without having teachers and students present in the same classroom. These conversations consider how traditional classroom practices are changed, enhanced, or compromised with technology.

Teaching Diversity: Diversity is an awareness of cultural difference that has transformed the contents of textbooks, inspired new teaching techniques, and changed the ways we research how students read, write, and learn. These conversations consider how we might incorporate more-inclusive approaches in the classroom and what problems and possibilities these approaches might hold.

Critical Theory in the Classroom: Theory, often taught as a separate course in the undergraduate and graduate English curriculum, is now being integrated into undergraduate classes in new ways, with, for example, students approaching the literature they read from a variety of critical perspectives. These conversations focus on how we include critical theory in our literature classes, for example, given our primary responsibility of helping students understand and appreciate literary texts.

Figure 3.1. Examples of current topics in education and teaching.

- **Listservs.** Your graduate program may provide a listserv for instructors, or you may wish to join one of the listservs in your English subfield. Ask faculty in your area for advice about which group to join.

- **Electronic Sites.** Electronic materials are available on a variety of Web sites, including those of textbook publishers, the National Council of Teachers of English, and individual English departments. Or, just do a search by topic—service learning, critical theory in the literature classroom, or teaching argumentation, for example.

- **Conferences.** Major English conferences such as those sponsored by the Modern Language Association, Conference on College Composition and Communication, and Association of Writers and Writing Programs include sessions on current issues affecting teaching, as will other scholarly conferences, as it is scholarship that often drives pedagogical change. But watch, too, for announcements of smaller conferences focused on particular aspects of pedagogy, such as service learning, teaching with technology, and approaches to teaching college literature.

- **Journals.** Scholarly and creative journals of all sorts are always of interest since scholarly issues affect teaching. But also look for journals devoted to pedagogy, such as *Pedagogy*, *Feminist Teacher*, and *Exercise Exchange*.

- **Books.** There are many books and collections on all current aspects of teaching in literature, composition, creative writing, and other subfields of English studies. Visit the Web sites of publishers of these books or stop by publisher exhibits at conferences to see what is available.

- **Professional Organizations.** Join professional organizations such as MLA, NCTE, AWP, TESOL, and the International Association of Teachers of English as a Foreign Language (IATEFL) to get updates on conferences, publications, and other professional matters related to teaching.

Gaining Teaching Credentials in Other Fields

Though we have emphasized how to gain teaching credentials in English studies, you might also consider developing a graduate minor in such adjacent areas as education, women's studies, black studies, American studies, or English as a second language. In choosing a minor area, you will likely find that you gravitate to certain fields based on your scholarly pursuits. Perhaps you are studying gender issues or feminist theory; then, of course, women's studies would be a logical extension of your interests. Gaining credentials in English as a second language (ESL) studies is particularly useful as many institutions now have increasing numbers of students who are nonnative speakers. These fields are often interdisciplinary and have programs or departments consisting entirely or partly of faculty whose disciplinary base is in English or another department. Thus, once on the job, you might find yourself teaching courses that are in some way cross listed in English and the other field and perhaps attending meetings and contributing to the growth of the other program or department. Pursuing a broader range of work can be intellectually stimulating to you both as a scholar and as a teacher, and the versatility may also increase your marketability when you search for an academic job. Many institutions are seeking instructors with a broad spectrum of teaching interests because it saves them from having to hire faculty with separate specialties. With even a cursory glance at the MLA Job List, you will notice how varied the many jobs and their qualifications are. So when applying for jobs, the additional qualifications of teaching in a minor field may give you the edge you need to compete successfully.

Demonstrating Teaching Excellence in the Job Search

In the academic job search, most students prepare a dossier of materials including a curriculum vita (academic résumé), letters of recommendation, and other materials that exemplify their work in teaching, scholarship, service, administration and/or editing. Sometimes the documentation for teaching takes the form of what is called a teaching portfolio— something we discuss more fully in Appendix B. In the nonacademic job search, too, you may want to build a dossier of supporting material that you can select from and then submit with your résumé to demonstrate your teaching ability. How can you prepare for this process? As we have stressed throughout this book, it is important during your graduate school years to reach out for as much teaching experience as you can and to become as proficient as possible.

Beyond simply obtaining experiences, it is also wise gradually to collect and assemble a variety of materials to document your teaching. We recommend that, early on, you set aside a folder in which to add artifacts as you acquire them. What kinds of documentation should you save? Following are just some possibilities.

- **Formal and Informal Student Evaluations and Surveys.** You can use these data to provide numerical summaries of your work ("My teaching evaluations are consistently high, averaging 4.7 on a 5 point scale") or discursive summaries ("One student remarked 'The comments on my work were so useful that I found myself revising extensively for the first time'"). Alternatively, you may include actual copies of your numerical evaluations or a typed list of discursive comments.

- **Observations of Your Teaching by Peers and Faculty.** When peers or faculty mentors observe your class, ask them to write up a formal page-long summary signed by them. These first-hand testimonials by others may be included in your dossier and can be added to your own self-evaluations.

- **Entries from Your Teaching Log.** Your teaching log likely contains many reflections on significant moments—perhaps your response to a difficult question in class or your concern about how to respond to a particular student's writing problem. The log, though likely not to appear in your dossier in its raw form, can still provide a wealth of detail for you to draw from both in writing reflective statements about your teaching and in preparing for job interviews.

- **Copies of Class Materials.** Actual syllabi, assignments, miscellaneous handouts, and samples of how you respond to student writing may be included in your dossier as examples of how you work. They may also be used to provide specific details for you to use to ground either a written reflective account of your teaching or to respond to job interview questions.

- **Copies of Class Materials for Proposed Courses.** Make up syllabi and other materials for courses that you think you might be asked to teach but have not yet actually taught, so that you can demonstrate your ability to develop a wide range of courses.

- **List of Teaching and Tutoring Assignments.** Keep track of all the courses you teach or assist in and any tutoring that you do, along with any teaching you do outside the academy. Without a record, it is easy to forget what you did and when you did it. However, with this record, you can construct an actual list of all your teaching assignments for your teaching portfolio.

- **List of Teaching-Related Publications and Presentations.** Keep track of any conference presentations, publications, or even local demonstrations or workshops on teaching you do for your department or program. Construct a summary for your teaching portfolio that will show both your disciplinary expertise and your awareness that teaching of all sorts has a scholarly basis.

- **Your Teaching Philosophy.** Your teaching philosophy will likely evolve over time, so we recommend that throughout graduate school you often revisit and refine your ideas about it. Acquire as much varied experience as you can and document it. Once you graduate, you can use this material in your dossier, as part of a formal statement of your philosophy, or in responding to job interview questions.

4 Establishing Yourself as a Scholar

Reading, writing, and mulling over ideas in depth is very much at the heart of English graduate work. That alluring prospect is probably what draws most people to graduate school initially and also what sustains them through the long days and nights. After all, for those who live the life of the mind anyway, what better way is there to spend time? If you are like us, you may have also been attracted to graduate school by images of the traditional scholar, researching alone for hours in quiet library archives and making important discoveries that would excite other scholars.

While we don't wish to shatter this image completely, we do want to encourage you, in this chapter, to think of scholarship in broader, more-contemporary terms. Certainly, scholarship in English these days can involve locating books and articles on areas of interest and sharing new ideas or insights with colleagues, but it rarely takes place only in library basements anymore. Instead it may be conducted electronically or collaboratively with other researchers, or its methodology may involve interviews, observations, or fieldwork. And because creative writing has become an academic discipline in its own right, many colleges and universities see "scholarship" as including not only traditional research and reporting but also creative writing of various kinds. Accordingly, throughout this chapter, we use the umbrella term *scholarship* to include a broad range of critical and creative professional work.

Of course, different kinds of schools define scholarship more or less broadly, according to their particular histories and missions. English departments at research universities tend to emphasize more traditional types of scholarly work, such as twenty-page articles with extensive literature reviews, while teaching-oriented universities often encourage conference presentations or shorter informal essays that draw connections between research and teaching. Schools also differ in the amount of scholarship they require and the types of forums they encourage for presentation and publication. Research-oriented universities often expect faculty to author a book, or, at the very least, several well-placed articles, chapters, or stories for tenure and promotion; teaching-oriented universities, because they typically require heavier teaching loads, expect fewer publications. Whether you are on the tenure track or teaching part time will also make a difference in the amount of scholarship required. Tenure-track faculty are expected to make contributions to multiple areas of university or college life—not just teaching. While part-time faculty often do present papers, publish, and serve on committees, they are usually only required to teach. Also, scholarly expectations and definitions can differ across subdisciplines. Some disciplines within English emphasize traditional researching and reporting forms; others are more open to personal reflection and experimental styles. Finally, the number of jobs available in your discipline will affect how you prepare yourself as a scholar. The fewer the jobs, the greater the competition; the greater the competition, the more scholarship typically required.

> The number of jobs available in your discipline will affect how you prepare yourself as a scholar. The fewer the jobs, the greater the competition; the greater the competition, the more scholarship typically required.

In graduate school, you need to begin the process of joining your field and developing scholarly credentials. For those of you planning an academic career, it is important to become a member of this scholarly community, both absorbing and contributing new knowledge—and the sooner the better. We recommend that as a graduate student you begin the process of joining professional organizations, attending and giving papers at conferences, applying for grants and fellowships, and sending out pieces for publication. Remember: whatever you learn to do as a graduate student will serve you well in both obtaining and keeping a tenure-track job, because the less time you have to spend learning the ropes, the more easily you can move toward earning tenure. If you think

you want a teaching position outside of higher
education (e.g., you'd like to teach high school
or in a tutoring center) or a job outside of
academia altogether, then you may simply want
to get as much diverse reading and writing
experiences as you can—especially if you will be
working with students or clients from diverse
literacy backgrounds. In short, as with other
professional areas, it will be important for you to
consider your long-term goals and to research
your discipline as you plan how to best prepare
yourself, as a scholar, for the position you desire.

> Remember: whatever you learn to do as a graduate student will serve you well in both obtaining and keeping a tenure-track job, because the less time you have to spend learning the ropes, the more easily you can move toward earning tenure.

This chapter encourages you to review your
long term career goals in order to consider the
kinds of scholarly experience you will need; to
be aware of the many ways to get scholarly
experience and credentials in graduate school
and beyond; and to learn how to demonstrate your scholarly potential
and achievement in your job search.

Review Your Long-Term Career Goals

As you did when you reviewed your long-term teaching goals in Chapter
3, think about the kind of career you ideally imagine for yourself in five,
ten, or twenty years. Imagine a continuum of academic contexts,
ranging from a highly selective research institution at which you would
be expected to have an extensive and ambitious scholarly agenda to a
typical community college, which would likely require no publication
for tenure and promotion, with varying amounts of scholarship at
institutions between the two extremes. If you imagine that the average
time before applying for tenure is six years, you can appreciate the
accelerated work pace that is required. If you are planning to seek a
nonacademic position, consider how much and what kind of research
you will need to do to make yourself an attractive job applicant or to
help you fine tune your career goals. Here are some questions to
consider as you review your goals:

- Do you genuinely enjoy doing scholarship in your field, and
  would you like to devote most of your time to it? What would be
  your ideal ratio of time spent on scholarly work—two-thirds, one-
  third, none?

- Can you imagine yourself working throughout your career mainly in a fairly narrow area of expertise and striving to become one of the top scholars in that area? Scholars at this level have names that are known, are often keynote speakers at conferences, and produce not only multiple books and collections throughout their scholarly lifetime but also publish multiple shorter works in leading journals and as book chapters in influential collections. These scholars often have ongoing long projects (such as books or collections) while producing multiple single pieces and delivering papers at conferences each year. They may eventually hold a special appointment called an endowed chairship, through which they may devote most of their time to scholarship. Their jobs are often at the most prestigious research institutions—perhaps Ivy League schools or other well-funded private schools, or state institutions in the "Big 10" with PhD programs.

- Would you like to devote considerable time to your scholarly work but at a slightly less-frenetic pace? Perhaps you imagine yourself producing one or two books or collections, along with multiple shorter works, over the course of your scholarly lifetime. In a typical year, you might produce one or two articles or chapters, while perhaps working on an ongoing larger project. You may wish to branch out into several scholarly areas and to strive to be known and respected in those areas. These jobs are found at a variety of research institutions and some comprehensive ones, either with PhD or MA granting programs.

- Would you like to devote nearly all your time to teaching with very little or even no publishing demands? If you are more interested in teaching, you may wish to spend only minimal time on scholarly work. You can see yourself keeping up with a few journals in your field and attending some conferences over time. Full-time positions like these may be found at community colleges and some small four-year colleges. Part-time adjunct positions—in almost any teaching context—also typically require minimal scholarship.

- Perhaps your primary reason for attending graduate school is to read and discuss literature, to become a creative or technical writer, or to learn more about theories of composition. If so, you should consider exploring the world of nonacademic jobs for which your general ability to analyze, write, and do research would be useful. Think about technical writing, grant writing, directing a nonprofit agency, editing, and a whole variety of other possibilities.

Identifying your scholarly preferences and abilities is vital as you envision your professional future. In our private moments of grandiosity, we may all wish to be paradigm breakers and scholars of the caliber of a Judith Butler, Andrea Lunsford, or John Ashberry. But does this really fit you? Perhaps you may wish instead to emulate your faculty mentors who are less glorified but still highly respected or to create some other balance of professional work. Our advice is to reach out for as much scholarly experience as you can while in graduate school, to explore and test your interests and capabilities in as many ways as you can, and to develop a scholarly agenda for yourself. All this experience can then be used for your job search, whether or not you wind up continuing to do scholarly work.

> Reach out for as much scholarly experience as you can while in graduate school, to explore and test your interests and capabilities in as many ways as you can, and to develop a scholarly agenda for yourself.

Common Types of Scholarship

If you are new to graduate school—or considering applying to a graduate program—you may not be familiar with the variety of scholarly activities in which academics participate. Described briefly below are some of the most common types. Because expectations vary across subdisciplines, you should ask professors or advisors in your area which professional activities are most typical in your particular field.

- **Conference Presentations.** At conferences, people speak in a variety of venues, including panels of three to four people who deliver formal papers, read selections of creative work, or give informal talks of twenty minutes or so; forums or roundtables in which a group of people each give brief talks of five minutes or less, generally designed to spark group discussion; or poster sessions in which each presenter creates a visual representation of a study or project and then stands by as conference goers circulate around the posters and ask questions.

- **Workshops.** In workshops, one or more workshop leaders typically create a variety of active learning exercises and discussion prompts for a group interested in exploring a particular topic. Workshops can be an hour long or stretch out for several days. They are often included on the programs for academic conferences.

- **Journal Articles/Essays.** Journals that appear several times a year, either in print or electronic form, typically contain several articles on topics of interest to a particular audience. The articles vary widely but may include such possibilities as formal accounts of research, theoretical speculation, or close readings of texts, to name a few. These short pieces are typically ten to thirty pages in length.

- **Reviews.** New works are constantly emerging in every subdiscipline. To help readers keep up with new and significant publications, journals, magazines, and newspapers often include brief descriptions and critiques of such works. These pieces may be a couple of paragraphs to several pages in length.

- **Book Chapters.** In academia, books are very often collections of essays or articles written by various authors, all typically exploring facets of the same general topic. If you contribute work to a collection, your contribution will be called a chapter. Chapters, like journal articles, are usually ten to thirty pages long.

- **Scholarly Monographs, Books, or Collections.** These three are examples of extended projects that may be several hundred pages in length. A book is likely to be published by a publishing company, whereas monographs are often in-house publications of centers, institutes, and programs. For a book, one or more authors write all the chapters, whereas a collection is overseen by one or more editors, with chapters usually written by any number of other contributors, perhaps including some written by the editor(s).

- **Poetry, Drama, Fiction, Literary Nonfiction.** If you are pursuing creative writing, these are the forms your work will most likely take. The most common publication venue is the literary magazine or journal. Magazines and journals differ (often greatly) in terms of the genre(s) they publish, the styles they encourage, and the preferred length of submissions. Another publishing venue is the literary anthology. Anthologies are edited collections of creative work that are often unified by a time period (e.g., *The Best American Poetry 2005*) or theme (e.g., *Golf's Best Short Stories*).

■ **Readings of Original Creative Work.** For creative writers, an alternative to the academic conference is often the public reading. At readings, writers typically preface and then read a selection of published work or work in progress. Readings may be focused on a single writer, or they may involve multiple writers. While some readings are open to any writer who wishes to participate, many are "invited." Invited readings, often sponsored by university departments or bookstores, are typically the result of a major accomplishment (e.g., prestigious publication, award) on the part of the writers involved.

It is from this range of what typically counts as scholarship that you will need to build your scholarly credentials.

Common Ways to Obtain Scholarly Experience

If you are like most students, you envision graduate school as a time to *acquire* knowledge—and, indeed, it is. But, in order to be competitive in a tough job market, you must also begin *producing* knowledge in the sorts of venues just described. Here are some ways to get started.

Learn as much as you can about scholarship from your seminars, courses, and the school library. If your department offers courses in research methods, scholarship in English, or academic or creative writing, by all means, take these courses. Or, if your school library offers short courses or workshops on primary or secondary research, be sure to sign up for them. Technological innovations have altered library research radically, and it is constantly changing, too, so if you don't make an effort to learn and to keep up, it will hamper your research efforts.

The projects you complete in your courses will offer another important way of learning about scholarship in your field. For most courses, you will be conducting secondary research, so pay attention to the tenor and textual conventions of the "scholarly conversation" you find happening among scholars as you research a particular topic. Think of your project as contributing to that conversation, whether it is ever published or not. Ask your professors for feedback that would help you revise your work for a conference presentation, or, perhaps, even for publication. And, use these writing opportunities to help you shape a foundation for thesis and dissertation work. Topics or themes for these important culminating projects often arise from ideas explored earlier in course papers.

Attend or create a research, scholarship, or writing group. Many graduate programs provide a variety of scholarly groups for students beyond the realm of formal courses. Most are scholarly reading and discussion groups in such areas as eighteenth-century literature, critical theory, or composition theory. These discussion groups can be an invaluable way to familiarize yourself with the scholarly conversation in an area, to read key pieces of writing, and to learn about conferences. If your department does not have any, you can always team up with a faculty member and start your own. Similarly, many departments have writing groups in which you can share your work in progress: conference papers, articles for publication, or creative writing. Ideally, such groups offer a way to get constructive feedback on your writing. They also provide opportunities to gain experience talking in front of a group and fielding questions afterward, thereby preparing for presenting at a conference. These writing groups, too, can be enormously helpful, so if one is not available, start your own. And, finally, you may wish to seek out or start your own thesis or dissertation support group in which members exchange and offer feedback on drafts of chapters. All these sorts of groups provide communities in which you can join the professional conversation.

> Discussion groups can be an invaluable way to familiarize yourself with the scholarly conversation in an area, to read key pieces of writing, and to learn about conferences.

Join the professional organizations most critical to your areas of scholarly interest. English Studies has large organizations such as MLA, NCTE, AWP, TESOL, and IATEFL and innumerable small organizations that focus on specific subjects such as the history of women in rhetoric or the writer Virginia Woolf. As a member of these organizations, you can stay abreast of announcements of conferences, publications, listservs, and other scholarly matters of interest.

Become familiar with the leading journals or other publishing venues in your subdiscipline. Experienced scholars always take time at least to skim the latest journals, both print and electronic, in order to "keep up with the field." Since new ideas are constantly being advanced, it is wise to get into this habit yourself. Some journals can be skimmed in your school or department library. Others you may wish to

> Experienced scholars always take time at least to skim the latest journals, both print and electronic, in order to "keep up with the field." Since new ideas are constantly being advanced, it is wise to get into this habit yourself.

subscribe to so that you will have them on hand in your own scholarly library. You might ask professors, too, if they have any back issues of journals that you could borrow.

Subscribe to the listservs in your areas of scholarly interest. Listservs exist for virtually every subdiscipline from eighteenth-century studies to creative writing pedagogy to writing program administration, as well as for the larger English discipline. Subscribers range from well-known scholars to graduate students. What kinds of discussion items might you see? The range can vary, including discussions of current issues in teaching and scholarship, recent publications, notices of conferences and publishing opportunities, commentary in the popular press, advice about professional matters, and even collaboration at the concrete level of locating lost colleagues or lost citations. What these listservs provide is a forum for ongoing scholarly discussions in an area. After all, a discipline or subdiscipline is never just a static body of knowledge but rather an ongoing and ever-changing conversation. As a subscriber, you will immediately stay abreast of this conversation. You should ask faculty or other graduate students for recommendations for the most useful and interesting listservs. Or, consult the following Web sites with links to a variety of English studies listservs:

- Voice of the Shuttle: http://vos.ucsb.edu/browse.asp?id =2976#id1685 for literature listservs
- Michigan State University: http://www.rhetoric.msu.edu/ graduate/listservs.html for rhetoric and composition listservs
- Ohio University: http://www-as.phy.ohiou.edu/~rouzie/569A/ compcreative/Listservs.htm for creative writing listservs and news groups.

Assist faculty with scholarly projects. Faculty often need assistance either with their personal scholarship or with research projects for the department or university. As a research assistant, you may help in a variety of ways. For example, you could find and compile citations for written sources and other research materials; conduct surveys, interviews, and observations; co-write proposals for grants and fellowships; provide clerical help by typing up notes, contacting research sources or study participants, or doing the "legwork" of procuring materials from libraries. Such possibilities are invaluable opportunities to see firsthand how an experienced scholar works and to familiarize yourself with both resources and methods. This experience can help you build the confidence you need to tackle your own projects. Either look for advertised research assistantships or simply ask faculty members informally if they need help with a project. In these arrangements, there may be funds available to pay you, or you may work out another option such as receiving one or two graduate credits in exchange for your work.

Plan for the conversion of your major scholarly projects into publishable form. The capstone of most graduate programs is a scholarly dissertation or collection of creative writing at the PhD level and sometimes a thesis or creative project at the MA or MFA level. These capstone experiences are intended to provide graduate students with the opportunity to produce an extended piece (or substantial collection) of writing, and, typically, are the culmination of several years of study. Whatever your particular subfield in English, you should begin envisioning your final project early on as you prepare for it—and try, too, imagining it not as finalized in its graduate school form but rather as work that can be revised for later publication. Do you have a conventional literature review chapter? Perhaps a later article will include only some of these citations. Do you have a collection of poems? Perhaps you will later revise some, cut others, and reconfigure them into a book. Do you have a dissertation that you think might become a book? Since the two are so different, more than likely, your present chapters will have to be dramatically reconfigured. In imagining converted versions of your work, it is always good to consult faculty members who know it well. Ask them for suggestions for the converted forms it might take. Survey similar publications, too, for other ideas. With this sort of projected plan, you will be in a strong position to articulate in job interviews what your further scholarly agenda will be. Furthermore, once past graduate school, you will be able to enact that agenda. Typically, assistant professors turn first to their dissertations or other capstone projects for material either to convert into a book or into several publishable articles or creative submissions. Those of you in areas of creative writing who are

> Whatever your particular subfield in English, you should begin envisioning your final project early on as you prepare for it—and try, too, imagining it not as finalized in its graduate school form but rather as work that can be revised for later publication.

not planning an academic career will still no doubt hope to publish a body of creative work, and your culminating project may form the basis for that.

You can pursue all these possibilities right within your own department as a part of your graduate study. However, at some point, you will want to move into a broader realm of scholarly forums. The next section describes ways to get started.

Getting Started in Scholarly Forums outside Graduate School

Presenting at Conferences and Giving Readings

Many graduate students begin their scholarly careers with a conference presentation. To find out about conferences in your discipline, start by asking your professors. Many graduate directors will post information about upcoming conferences (usually called "conference calls") or distribute such information over e-mail. Take a look, too, at recent issues of journals in your field. Many journals include conference announcements within the final few pages of an issue. You might also try searching the Web sites of professional organizations in your discipline. Organizations such as MLA, NCTE, AWP, TESOL, and IATEFL have helpful Web pages that include current information on conferences. Be sure to investigate ways to defray the cost of attending a conference. If other graduate students are also going, plan to share a room in the conference hotel or book a room at a cheaper hotel nearby. See if your department or institution has funds to contribute to your travel or lodging.

As a first step to presenting at a conference, it is wise to attend a few in your field. Consider these tips.

- Pay attention to the topics discussed and the presentation formats used.
- If a presenter whose talk you enjoy says he or she has copies of the paper, take one. After all, the best way to write a successful conference paper of your own is to study how others do it.
- Try to determine if a conference accepts the work of graduate students and, if so, the ballpark percentage of them invited to participate.
- If you know upfront that a particular conference tends to invite mostly distinguished scholars—and that it's a rare graduate

student who makes the cut—consider trying a more student-friendly conference at first.

As you might imagine, the more competitive the conference, the harder it may be to get accepted. If you want to build confidence, start with less-competitive or local conferences.

Submitting a Proposal

Once you have identified an appropriate conference, you can begin the process of submitting a proposal. Most conferences require that an abstract—some an actual paper—be submitted. Before trying your hand at abstract writing, you will need to find out what the conventions are for the conference in which you are interested.

> If you know upfront that a particular conference tends to invite mostly distinguished scholars—and that it's a rare graduate student who makes the cut—consider trying a more student-friendly conference at first.

- Will you only need to write an abstract, or will you have to submit an entire paper?
- How long should your submission be?
- Should you send multiple copies?
- Should you leave your name on your abstract or paper, or does the conference use "blind review" (i.e., reviewers read all submissions without knowing who the respective authors are)?

Some of this information can be found in the conference call; some is part of the tacit knowledge that you'll need to learn on your own as you become a member of your discipline. The best approach to take is to ask lots of questions—of professors, peers, and conference organizers, if possible. Also, try to get copies of actual abstracts that have been accepted. If you look at a number of abstracts that have worked for a particular conference, you will start to see a pattern in common (e.g., review of current literature, statement of a problem and its significance, description of proposed presentation).

Getting Rejected

If your proposal is *not* accepted, don't despair. Everyone in your field probably has had a proposal rejected at one time or another. Perhaps there were simply many more proposals than there were places on the program. Perhaps your ideas did not match the conference needs as well as those of others. Or, perhaps you simply need to sharpen your ideas further. Whatever the reason for rejection, you will still gain much from undergoing the process, and you can use this experience to your advantage the next time. Just remember the old adage "Nothing ventured; nothing gained" and persevere.

Getting Accepted

If your paper *is* accepted, find out what the presentation expectations are and stick to them. For example, most conferences will specify how long your presentation should be. Nothing is more irritating (to other presenters and audience members alike) than the presenter who is allotted fifteen minutes of a session but takes thirty. Another expectation of conference papers is that they be relevant and professional. If your presentation is based on work you are doing for a graduate course or in close consultation with a faculty member outside of class, chances are good that it will be relevant to the conference selection committee and an audience in your field. To make your presentation professional, write and revise it with input from others. If you have a group before whom you can practice delivering your paper, by all means, do so. This presentation provides you with a low-risk trial run. Your audience can offer valuable feedback on improving your delivery style and on any points in the paper that are not clear. They can ask you the sorts of questions ahead of time that audiences generally ask after a paper is delivered, thereby helping you gain experience at fielding queries. Realize that a conference paper, because it is typically heard and not read by the audience, needs to be written for listeners. It's a good idea to try to make your points as clear as possible through such means as repetition of key words or ideas, summary statements, and, if you are able, visual aides.

> Everyone in your field probably has had a proposal rejected at one time or another. . . . You will still gain much from undergoing the process, and you can use this experience to your advantage the next time.

At the Conference

Once at the conference at which you will deliver your paper, be sure to arrive at your session's room a few minutes early. Typically, you will have a chance to meet your session chair who may ask you for a few biographical facts so that he or she can introduce you, if you have not already been contacted by that person before the conference. A typical panel includes several speakers followed by a question-and-answer session. Most people are a bit nervous at their very first presentation, so don't worry if you feel this way, too. Just go thoroughly prepared (having practiced your paper out loud), get plenty of rest the night before, be on time, dress appropriately, and plan on enjoying the experience of having your ideas considered seriously by a group of colleagues.

> Most people are a bit nervous at their very first presentation, so don't worry if you feel this way, too. Just go thoroughly prepared . . . and plan on enjoying the experience of having your ideas considered seriously by a group of colleagues.

Giving Readings

While many creative writing students do participate in conferences, it is also very common for them to pursue opportunities to read their creative work to an audience rather than present a paper (as mentioned earlier). Readings are sometimes incorporated into scholarly conferences and often require a submission of work that is reviewed before an invitation is extended. More commonly, though, readings are organized by a department, creative-writing program, or local business (e.g., bookstore or coffee shop) to promote student work, and the program as a whole.

If you are interested in gaining public reading experience, you will want to keep your eyes and ears open for public readings that are in the planning stages and to approach organizers about the possibility of participating. This tactic will work best if the reading is informal and local (e.g., a student/faculty reading event in your department) or huge and very public (e.g., a poetry-reading marathon at the local coffee shop). Most departments/programs try to include as many students as possible in the readings they sponsor. Local businesses, though, tend to depend on recommendations from others (e.g., program directors, professors, established local writers, well-known patrons) when deciding who to include in readings. Remember, no matter what the particular venue, participation in readings is good experience—and a good way to get your name out into the local creative writing community.

> No matter what the particular venue, participation in readings is good experience—and a good way to get your name out into the local creative writing community.

If you are invited to read in a public forum, you will want to prepare beforehand by carefully selecting work that a listening audience will appreciate; by writing brief prefaces to help frame or contextualize your work for listeners; and by practicing the reading, so you know how much you can read in the time provided.

Submitting Work for Publication

By the time they finish their program, many graduate students will have more conference presentations than publications, but it is still advisable at least to start the process of submitting written work for publication while still in graduate school. The tips that follow offer you a good place to begin.

- Become familiar with the venues for publication in your discipline.
  - What is the range of journals publishing in your area?
  - If you have a book-length project, what publishing companies are most likely to publish it?
  - Are there electronic sites for your writing?
- Visit all the Web sites for publishing venues, browse through varied examples of published work, and stop by the publishing displays at any conference you attend.
- If there is a publishing directory for your discipline, make sure to get a copy of it. (One example of this type of publication is the *International Directory of Little Magazines and Small Presses* for creative writers.)
- When you have identified potential publishing venues, gather information about submission processes and requirements.

Below we provide a general overview of the processes for publishing a variety of scholarly work.

Submitting Journal Articles and Book Reviews

Target Submissions.   As you peruse journals in your field, start becoming aware of how varied they are and how they differ from one another. As you survey them, notice, in particular, how they differ in focus, style, scope, and prestige. As with conferences, you may wish to start by submitting work to a less-competitive journal (acceptance percentages for journals can often be found on their Web sites) or a journal that is devoted to publishing student work, such as *The Sigma Tau Delta Review*, sponsored by the well-known English honor society.

But you must also target your work to the most appropriate forum, so make sure your work fits in with a publication's usual material. Read over the journal's "submission guidelines" (usually found in the opening pages or screens of the journal) for information on how to submit your work. Not only will this material likely specify the journal's area of interest, but it will also provide information such as the preferred approach, length, and documentation style. Pay attention to any announcements of special thematic issues coming up for which your work might be appropriate.

Then begin to look at any seminar projects that you might convert into something of publishable quality. You might seek the advice of faculty mentors on whether a paper looks promising and where they think it might be well placed, or you could run it by a writing group in which you participate. If you've given a version of your work as a conference paper that was well received, that, too, can provide encouragement for you to expand the work. Or, you may have completed a thesis or dissertation chapter, which, with revision, could serve as a stand-alone article. Whatever piece you choose, be sure to get plenty of feedback on the draft you plan to send, so that you submit your strongest possible work.

Preparing the Submission.   Once you are ready to submit a piece, be sure to follow all editorial directions carefully, including such seemingly small matters as the number of copies required, whether to include your name on the actual piece, whether to include a return stamped envelope, and what typeface to use. Most people include a brief cover letter, which provides an overview of the submission (e.g., what the central argument is and why it's important) and thorough and accurate contact information. The letter here offers an example.

Dear Professor Anderson,

I am enclosing an article titled "A Self by Any Other Name: Recovering Historical Voice(s)." Perhaps no contemporary discussions are more important for feminist rhetorical theory than contentious postmodern debates about the terms ethos, persona, and voice, in which the very possibility of agency is questioned. "Coming to voice" has, for years, been identified as a key rhetorical act for women writing and speaking. In my article, I outline key tropes used historically by women rhetors to express ethos, represent a persona, or find voice. This historical overview includes descriptions of both the roles that women have chosen for themselves, as well as the rhetorical representations of them by others.

Currently, I am a graduate student at the University of _____, where I am finishing my dissertation in this area. A previous version of this piece was well received at the _____ conference.
Thank you for your consideration. I look forward to hearing from you soon.
Sincerely,
[student name]

The convention is to submit a particular piece to only one journal at a time. However, you may send other pieces to other journals, too, so keep track of what submission is where. Expect a turnaround time of anywhere from a few weeks to many months. The publishing pipeline is clogged nowadays, so it is not uncommon for there to be long delays. If, at some point, you wish to know where your piece is in the process, it is perfectly appropriate to send a polite inquiry to the editor, perhaps by e-mail.

The Internal Publishing Process.   What happens to your paper once the journal receives it? Refereed journals distribute the piece to two or more readers who review it carefully, judging it for overall quality and appropriateness. They give their recommendations to their editor who makes the final decision. With nonrefereed journals, the editor will often make the decision. When you hear from the editor, the verdict will likely be that it is rejected, accepted with revisions, or accepted as is.

- If the article is rejected, read the comments carefully and see if you can glean clues for how to revise and submit it elsewhere. Try not to take the rejection personally and, above all, don't let it deter you from trying again. Everyone has pieces rejected from time to time, so try to develop a thick skin; call it a learning experience and persevere.

- If the article is accepted provided you revise it according to editorial suggestions, then try to address all the requested changes. You may find aspects of the piece that you don't wish to change; if so, you may certainly indicate why you would rather not change them, possibly initiating a conversation with the editor. But, otherwise, try to approach the revision task in a spirit of open-mindedness and cooperation. The editors and reviewers are experienced professionals whose advice will, often as not, strengthen your piece. Return your revised work within the time frame indicated by the editor, along with a cover letter detailing your responses to the requested changes.

- If the article is accepted as is—rejoice! Overall, few pieces are given such a green light, and even these may have a few minor issues to address.

Once your piece comes out in print, you will receive a copy of the issue in which it appears. In the meantime, save all of the correspondence along the way.

Book Reviews.   Whereas articles are based on your own scholarly work, book reviews offer overviews of someone else's work. Many journals assign their reviews, while others accept open submissions. So look at samples of reviews to get ideas for how to write them. It is always a good idea to send an editor a letter of inquiry first if you would like to submit a review.

Submitting Poems, Stories, Essays, and Plays to Journals, Magazines, and Anthologies

The process for submitting creative writing to literary journals and magazines is very similar to the article-submission process. You should familiarize yourself with a wide range of journals and obtain a copy of *The International Directory*, or a like publication, to determine where your work has the best chance of being accepted. Follow the submission guidelines, available on the inside cover of the journal or on the publication's Web site, and include a cover letter that briefly describes the contents. It is also customary to provide a brief biography, which mentions where you attend school and names of other publications, if you have them. Here is an example:

Dear Adam Young,
I am enclosing three poems for your consideration: "Ocean Way," "On the Beach," and "Waterworks."
Currently, I am a graduate student at the University of _____, where I teach introductory courses in creative writing and composition. My publications include poems in _____ and short stories in _____. I recently won my university's Graduate Poetry Contest.
Thank you for your consideration. I look forward to hearing from you soon.
Sincerely,
[student's name]

Submitting to anthologies of shorter creative works is different, because you will usually be responding to a published advertisement, or "call," from the editors rather than sending your work in unsolicited. Keep in mind that anthologies often have themes (e.g., nature, spirituality) that guide the editors' selection process.

One important difference between the article-submission and the creative-writing submission process is the type of response you will receive. Usually, responses to articles will come in the form of a personal letter to the author, which not only explains whether the work has been accepted, but why it has (or hasn't) been accepted. The letter also often includes excerpts from reviewer responses, if not copies of the reviews themselves. Responses to creative-writing submissions are usually very short form letters, especially if the work has been rejected. If an editor can't publish the work at that time, but is interested in seeing more, he or she will often write an encouraging handwritten note on the short form letter. This is all to say that you should not get discouraged by the small slips of paper returned with your submissions; everyone gets them!

Submitting Chapters to Collections

Collections are books on a designated topic for which many writers have contributed essays. Often the editor(s) of a collection will issue a "call for papers" describing the focus of the collection and asking for submissions. These calls may appear in journals, on listservs, and on bulletin boards at conferences, among other places. Or, someone may know that you are doing work in a particular area and simply invite you to submit a chapter.

If the editors have a clear vision for their final product, they may ask for an actual chapter draft. If they don't, they may just ask for an abstract of a potential chapter. Then they will choose those abstracts that look most promising and seem to fit together well. As with other types of submissions, follow all directions, meet the stated deadline, be cooperative, and keep track of where the collection is in its process. Your chapter will be rejected, accepted with revision, or just accepted as is. An abstract may be accepted, with some guidance on how the chapter should be developed, or it may be rejected outright. If your piece is accepted, you will find that the entire process of getting the collection published may take several years, as the collection editors negotiate contracts, publisher reviews, and several levels of editing. Once published, you should receive a copy of the collection.

Submitting Proposals for Collections and Books

Collection Idea. If you have an idea for a collection and would like to edit or co-edit one, first investigate the possible publishers who might be interested in this area.

- Talk to prospective editors through e-mail or at conferences, or, if a publishing representative is on campus, you may ask that person to pass your idea along to his or her acquisitions editor.
- Write up a call for papers, advertise, and, once chapter proposals arrive, sort through them.
- Assemble a formal collection proposal, including the abstracts, and submit it to a publisher. Most publishers post proposal guidelines on their Web sites to guide authors and editors through this process. (Consult the chapter bibliography in Appendix A for more information on collection and book proposals.)

If your idea is rejected, you can submit it to other places. With collection proposals, it is acceptable to send the same proposal to several publishers simultaneously. Only when you sign a contract do you need to give that company exclusive rights to your work. If your idea is accepted, you may be told to turn in a manuscript before being awarded a contract, or you may be given a preliminary contract. From there, the project will proceed through the stages to final publication, a process that may take several years.

Idea for a Book. If you have an idea for a single- or coauthored book, the general process is similar, but the specifics may differ according to your subfield. Perhaps your dissertation (or another substantial piece of work) has the potential to become a book. (Some resourceful graduate students have even made their dissertation proposals double as book proposals.) Investigate possible publishers; run preliminary ideas by editors of publishing companies; write up a prospectus if required; and submit it to publishers. (Some publishers sponsor first-book contests for creative writers.) From there, the project will proceed through stages similar to that of a collection.

Other Possibilities. All of these forms of publication are possibilities for graduate students. More than likely, longer collection and book projects will just get underway in graduate school and be completed while you are on the job. But you may also have articles, chapters, and individual poems/stories/plays in varying spots along the publishing pipeline at any given time.

Honors, Grants, Fellowships, and Residencies

Honors are forms of recognition for which other people, generally faculty, nominate you. For example, you may be nominated for producing the best dissertation of the year in your department or for having passed your oral exam at an exemplary level. If you are fortunate enough to have your work recognized in this way, be sure to keep records of those honors, as well as other grants and fellowships you may receive. Grants and fellowships are sources of money that you can apply for to finance your scholarly work.

Grants and Fellowships

As a graduate student, you can use money from grants and fellowships to cover any number of scholarly needs—attending a conference; buying computers, books, and other materials; serving as seed money so that you can develop an idea; and traveling to conduct primary or secondary research. Once you become a faculty member, you may also use it to pay for a research assistant for yourself or to pay for someone to teach courses you are assigned to teach so that you have time to write. Fellowships, in particular, include stipends that often allow extended time for research. The available sums for individual research projects in English generally vary from a few hundred dollars to several thousands. In some subfields such as rhetoric and composition, however, large projects of educational significance, perhaps including several researchers and even several institutions, can bring in considerably more.

More than this, getting grant and fellowship awards is an important expectation in many careers, particularly academic ones. So, the sooner you begin learning this process, the better. Find opportunities by asking mentors and other graduate students and by searching Web sites, listservs, bulletin boards, notices in journals, and ads in the *Chronicle of Higher Education* or similar publications. As with other publishing activities, you must learn as much as you can about the grant or fellowship guidelines, choose appropriate possibilities that match your work, and submit a proposal after looking at successful samples and seeking out lots of feedback from your mentors. (See the chapter resources in Appendix A for further information.)

Writing Residency

For a creative writer, an equivalent to the fellowship is the writing residency. Foundations and arts centers across the country offer writers, artists, and composers the opportunity to compete for short (e.g., as little as two weeks) or extended (up to several months) stays in a retreatlike setting (often termed "artist colony') to do their work. Some of these residencies (especially those offered by the most well-endowed programs) cover all room and board expenses (i.e., you pay only your travel-related and miscellaneous costs). Others will pay a portion of room and board and ask for a small per-diem payment to cover the difference.

Application Process. The application process generally involves submitting a sample of creative work and an overview of what you plan to accomplish if you are awarded a residency. Foundation/program board members then review submissions and make selections. Residencies, like fellowships, are often very competitive, though most programs are open to new, yet-to-be established writers.

Demonstrating Scholarly Excellence in the Job Search

In the academic job search, your dossier will include a variety of materials that demonstrate your scholarly experiences and abilities. These materials include details in your curriculum vita about conference presentations, readings, and publications; honors, grants, and fellowships received; samples of your writing; and letters of recommendation by faculty familiar with your work. If you are planning to conduct a job search outside the academy, your dossier will likely include a résumé, along with selected samples of your writing. A piece of well-researched writing done in a seminar; flyers and brochures written on an administrative job; or the text of a grant you wrote—these are just a few examples of how graduate school experience can be used as evidence of what you can do on a nonacademic job. How can you prepare for either type of job search? The first step, as we have stressed throughout this chapter, is to learn as much as you can and to reach out for as much experience as possible. Then, beyond that, you need to document all your scholarly activities. Keep a file folder of artifacts and jot down everything you do, so that when you prepare your dossier or résumé, everything will be at hand. There is a link between the outreach for experience and the documentation of it, for one expression we often repeat to our students is "It's another line on your vita." If, as a student, you continue to reach out for experience and to document it as you go along, you will find that you will have a surprisingly substantial vita or

résumé at the end of your graduate program. Here are some possibilities for documenting and collecting your work:

- **Log all of your scholarly efforts.** On separate sheets of paper,
note all presentations, published work, and honors/grants/
fellowships received. For each of these three main categories,
maintain your list in reverse chronological order—that is, with
your most recent activity first. In these lists, note not just the
activities that are completed but also those in process. For
example, you may have submitted a conference abstract that has
not yet been accepted, or perhaps it has been accepted but the
conference has not yet occurred. This meticulous record keeping
will serve you well come the time you prepare your dossier;
otherwise, much of the details of your work will likely slip your
memory. Bear in mind, too, that since you are just starting out,
you can round out your account with such activities as professional meetings, workshops, and conferences attended or
conference sessions you may have chaired, even if you didn't
present a paper.

- **Keep copies of all written or electronic materials.** Collect
copies of conference presentations; published print or electronic
works; manuscripts-in-progress; thesis or dissertation chapters;
and even outstanding seminar papers. Make sure all are neat and
letter perfect in an accessible folder. During your job search, you
may be asked to send samples of your scholarly work, so if you
already have some on hand and in good shape, it will simplify
your preparation. For those of you seeking academic positions,
once you receive an offer to visit a campus for an extended
interview, you may also need to prepare a piece of writing for a
presentation or reading. The materials that you have accumulated can serve as components of that writing.

- **Write descriptions of scholarly activities with which you
assisted faculty.** If you have held any formal or informal
research assistantships, be sure to write up brief job descriptions
detailing all you did and any results from that project—including
publications, grants, or other awards—while the experience is
still fresh in your memory. This information will help round out
your curriculum vita or résumé.

- **Draft your scholarly agenda.** Throughout your graduate
career, we recommend that you begin to formulate your schol-

arly agenda, regardless of whether you envision yourself producing one work a year or a dozen. What is this agenda? Experienced scholars will tell you that one project often builds upon another. At any time, we may have several projects in differing stages of completion—perhaps putting the finishing touches on a book, while also drafting an article or short story, and collecting materials and applying for grants for the next project. In addition, we are constantly on the lookout for ideas at conferences, on listservs, and in journals. Most often we can project activities at least a couple of years ahead, if not more. Get into these habits and you will find that your scholarly agenda takes shape.

How does this agenda-setting habit help you once on the job market? For those of you searching for an academic job, you will find that in your dossier and at job interviews you will be asked to articulate your scholarly agenda—what you plan to accomplish (in terms of research, presentations, and publications, for example) and your ideal deadlines for meeting these goals. And, incidentally, you will probably do so again every year thereafter—on annual reports of activity and on applications for tenure and promotion. For those of you searching for a nonacademic job, you will also likely be asked to project your plans several years into the future based on the evidence you present. If you are applying for a job in corporate writing that requires you to develop public relations materials, for example, you might be asked about the range of public relations writing you wish to do someday. Or, if you are applying to be an editor for a small journal, you might also be asked about your plans for upcoming creative projects—especially if it is a priority that a publication's editors also be working writers. So begin now to informally jot down your "big picture"—the directions and patterns that make your work coherent—with reference to past, present, and future projects.

> How can you prepare for either type of job search? The first step, as we have stressed throughout this chapter, is to learn as much as you can and to reach out for as much experience as possible.

- **Save copies of materials for writers of recommendation letters.** An important part of your dossier includes letters of recommendation written by faculty and other mentors. These letters, written by experienced members of your discipline and vouching for your accomplishments and potential, are critical. Though you likely won't ask for the letters until you begin preparing for your actual job search, start immediately not only to identify possible letter writers but also to collect materials documenting your activities and accomplishments for them. Set aside a file to save copies of seminar projects you complete in their courses, along with any other significant course work. Keep related samples of writing, too, such as conference papers or publications that spun off from those original seminar projects. Have a curriculum vita- or résumé-in-progress that you can polish up at any moment and a brief coherent overview of your scholarly agenda. This way, once you do ask for recommendations, you can provide your chosen writers with a small packet of supporting materials. Not only will the packet jog their memory, but it will offer them a rich source of detail on which they can draw in writing your letter.

5 Establishing Other Academic Selves: Service, Administration, Editing

While the experiences you gain as a teacher and scholar in graduate school should help you secure—and succeed in—the position you desire, you will want to make sure you develop skills in other areas valued by employers. A quick look through any of the well-known academic job lists will show you just how multi-faceted academic positions have become. As we mentioned in Chapter 1, it is now very common for position announcements to highlight qualifications and abilities in areas outside of teaching and scholarship.

Because the work of universities and their departments includes much more than just classroom instruction and research, hiring departments often look for applicants who can chair committees, jump-start a new major program, run a writing center, or edit a scholarly journal. Similarly, many nonacademic employers are eager to hire people who can handle a wide variety of responsibilities, including organizing community-service events, supervising a new project or initiative, or writing the company newsletter. And, as we suggested in Chapter 2, any employer wants to hire people who are well organized and collegial—two important abilities that are often developed through extracurricular professional activities.

Activities outside of teaching and research can also help you build the credentials you will need if you decide to start your own business after graduate school. Many people with strong English backgrounds, including extensive writing and editing experience, start their own writing/consulting/editing services as another alternative to the traditional academic career path. Besides the practical benefits, extracurricular professional activities—whether they are offered within your graduate program or sponsored by an outside department or agency—can be a lot of fun. They provide opportunities to discover hidden talents, develop new interests, and build lifelong professional relationships.

With this chapter, then, we hope to expand your definition of *professional development* to include the full range of learning opportunities that will help you round out your graduate-school experience and meet the multiple, diverse requirements of the professional positions you will most likely apply for after graduation. We've grouped these opportunities into three broad categories: service, administration, and editing. Because graduate programs vary with respect to how they address students' professional-development needs, we've included examples of both formal and informal means for gaining experience in these areas. Again, as you read this chapter, keep in mind your personal career goals and consider which of the opportunities discussed will best help you meet those goals.

Review Your Long-Term Career Goals

As you did when you reviewed your long-term teaching and research goals in previous chapters, think about the kind of position you can imagine yourself in and the amount and type of service, administration, and/or editing you would ideally like to do or could consider doing. Here are some questions to help you review:

- Do you really enjoy service, administration, and/or editing, and would you like to devote most, if not all, of your working life to it? (These positions can be found in many nonacademic contexts and within the academy in both upper administration—the realm of deans, provosts, and presidents—as well as in all of the accompanying administrative support programs such as student services and advising.)

- Would you like a position that includes a substantial amount of service and administration but also allows you to teach and do scholarly work? (These jobs are plentiful in English departments. Writing program administrators and department chairs, for example, typically devote a third to one-half of their time to service and administration.)

- Would you prefer a position with little or no service, administration, or editing? (Professorial positions at all kinds of universities involve only minimal work of this type. Most of your time would be devoted to teaching and scholarship.)

Gaining Service Experience

Shown here are two typical advertisements for positions that have a service component.

Excerpt of Advertisement A

Generalist position with experience teaching composition and survey courses in American and/or World Literature. Responsibilities: Teach four courses per semester; Advise and mentor students; Participate in universitywide committees; Teach in diverse delivery modes; Assist in department sponsored student publications and/or organizations; Engage in research. (HigherEdJobs.com 4/8/05. Accessed 5/16/05)

Excerpt of Advertisement B

Assistant Professor of Professional Writing to teach business/technical writing, advanced professional communication, print and online document design, and graduate courses in composition theory or practicum in college teaching. . . . We expect the person who fills the position to pursue an active research agenda resulting in scholarly publications in refereed journals and/or other respected venues. Participation in appropriate levels of service for the department, college, university and your profession will be expected, through contributions at the local, state and national levels. (HigherEdJobs.com 9/16/04. Accessed 5/16/05).

In academia, the term *service* is traditionally used to represent an array of activities that are expected of faculty—most typically of faculty members who have full-time appointments. As the above ads from recent job lists suggest, the term usually refers to work done on departmental or university committees, but it can also include extracurricular activities such as planning or facilitating a brown-bag discussion series, being a guest lecturer in a colleague's class, or organizing the annual picnic for English majors. Service can also include work done outside of the department or university, in the local community, for example, or nationally, for a professional organization.

Serving on Department Committees

One of the most obvious opportunities for gaining service experience in English departments is committee membership. Because it is just too difficult for all members of a department (especially a large department) to gather together regularly to discuss every question, issue, or problem that arises, much of a typical department's work is accomplished in committees. Most departments have numerous committees dedicated to various academic programs and initiatives, including, for example, first-year writing, general education, assessment, promotion/tenure of faculty, and graduate studies. Committees focused on nonacademic concerns, such as faculty/student social events, public relations, or equipment purchase/allocation are also quite common. Usually, "standing committees" (those that focus on ongoing issues or long-term projects) meet regularly (e.g., once or twice each month) to discuss concerns, make decisions, and draft proposals or reports for departmental consideration. If a pressing issue arises (e.g., the dean asks for a report on the possible effects of raising the enrollment cap on introductory courses—ASAP), a committee may meet more often—until the issue is resolved. "Ad hoc committees" (those that are formed to address an immediate or short-term concern) typically meet more frequently over a shorter period of time (e.g., a few months or one year only). One example would be a group of graduate-studies faculty that forms to research and discuss the possibility of adding a new graduate program or major.

Of course, while committee opportunities may abound in your department or program, it may seem difficult for you, as a student, to serve on one. Not surprisingly, most departmental committees are restricted to faculty because they address business that directly affects faculty lives (e.g., tenure issues, leadership concerns, curriculum revision/oversight). In fact, much is discussed in these committees that students needn't know (e.g., why the process for submitting promotion applications is different this year) and probably shouldn't know (e.g., who will get teaching assistantships and why). Some departmental committees, however, do offer graduate students—especially PhD students—the chance to participate. Committees that address issues related to first-year teaching (which many graduate students do) or the graduate program in general will often reserve committee seats for students. If this is the case in your department and you feel you would benefit from such service, find out how students get on the committees. Are they appointed? Elected? Do they simply volunteer?

Serving on Institutional and Disciplinary Committees

If opportunities for service on departmental committees are scarce at your school, you will want to investigate other possible options. One of these options is a collegewide or university committee. Though most of these committees are composed of faculty and staff members, some allow—and even encourage—student membership. Committees that focus on issues related to first-year undergraduate students (e.g., a student-retention committee, first-year experience committee, developmental education committee) often welcome the perspectives of graduate students who are teaching the writing, literature, or general-orientation courses required of undergraduates. Committees dedicated to graduate education (e.g., a university graduate committee or advisory board) also frequently include graduate-student representatives.

Still other options exist outside of the department or university. Local chapters or "affiliates" of professional academic organizations, such as NCTE, MLA, AWP, and TESOL, often form committees to plan a local conference or to organize events for a national conference being held in the area. National organizations themselves often offer the chance for student members to join issue-oriented caucuses or special-interest groups. To learn more about such possibilities, talk with your graduate adviser or a professor in your discipline. Better yet, contact the organizations themselves (most have Web sites with e-mail links to local affiliate groups) and ask about opportunities for graduate-student involvement.

Other Formal Service Opportunities

In addition to committee work, you will want to consider the many other service opportunities available to you. Your department may support a special collection or archive of works by a well-known author, for example. Often, volunteers are needed to catalog information, update Web sites, or publicize special events. At both the regional and national levels, editors of scholarly journals look for good manuscript reviewers and often contact graduate faculty to get names of bright students who would be interested in such work. If this type of service appeals to you, let your professors know so that when they are asked to recommend, they think of you. Finally, at the national level, textbook publishers often invite graduate students (especially those who have teaching assistantships) to read and respond to new editions of books for introductory courses. Though the publishers typically pay reviewers, the payment is usually minimal enough (e.g., $50 to $100) to be considered more of an honorarium than an actual dollar-per-hour payment, which is why you can consider it as service. Aside from gaining service credentials, these experiences help you build connections with editors and publishing representatives who may, in the future, seek you out to serve on an editorial board or write a textbook.

Informal Service Opportunities

If the more formal service opportunities discussed above seem elusive, consider the many informal ways to gain service credentials. Most graduate programs have graduate-student organizations whose purposes include creating community through social events, supporting the professional development needs of members, and/or advocating for better working conditions for teaching assistants. Instead of sitting on a formal committee, you might consider joining a student organization of this type and taking an active part in programs and events. For example, you might agree to organize a fund-raiser, such as a book sale or read-a-thon. You could also volunteer to be an officer for the organization. Almost all of these organizations need a president, secretary, and treasurer and are typically very open to potential officers whose enthusiasm makes up for any lack of on-the-job experience.

Many other informal service opportunities arise more organically, when a student sees a need in a program or department and then takes the initiative to address that need. Here are some common examples:

- Coordinating student or faculty research forums
- Organizing study groups
- Participating in peer mentoring initiatives
- Reviewing and reporting on new textbooks to teaching colleagues
- Making presentations on your area of expertise in a professor's class
- Starting a listserv or moo for your major program.

All of these activities can be considered under the umbrella term *service*.

Gaining Administrative Experience

As with service, administrative work in academia is plentiful, varied—and often expected of faculty at some point in their careers. The more common forms of administration within English departments include:

- Program development (e.g., designing a new major or concentration)
- Management (e.g., chairing the department; directing the undergraduate [or graduate] program; running a writing program or writing center; coordinating an annual visiting-lecturer series; running a poets-in-the-schools program)
- Supervision (e.g., overseeing graduate-teaching assistants or part-time instructors)

Another growing administrative area is assessment, for which faculty are hired specifically to help design and coordinate evaluations of programs, courses, and special initiatives.

Until quite recently, much academic administrative work was considered as "service." It has been difficult for colleges and universities to expand their notion of the "big three" realms of faculty life (research, teaching, and service) to include administrative activities, which often overlap with these three areas but have their own distinct characteristics. To initiate a new graduate program, for example, a faculty member would need to study similar programs at other schools (akin to traditional research, but not quite the same); educate other faculty about the possibilities (similar to teaching, but again not the same thing); and organize meetings to vote on program description, curriculum, and so on (much like service). However, as more and more faculty are hired expressly to do administrative work, contracts stipulate the amount and kind of administration to be done, the specific stipend or other reimbursement (e.g., reduced teaching responsibility), and how it will be considered in tenure/promotion review. And as contracts have begun to include specific mention of such work and to acknowledge the time and money required, it has taken on a life separate from service.

As you think about your overall career goals, you will want to consider how much administrative work you want to do, how much may be expected of you, and whether you have the personality to do it. While only you can decide how much administrative work you desire, we can tell you that, if you choose an academic path, the expectations for administration may depend upon your subfield within English. Though job ads for literature and creative-writing faculty sometimes mention administration (e.g., program development or coordination), ads for composition and rhetoric faculty regularly include an administrative component. In her "century's end" study of market trends in composition and rhetoric, for example, Gail Stygall found that 33 percent of the composition and rhetoric positions advertised in 1998 included some form of administration—nearly a 10 percent increase since 1994 (386). Our own analysis of the most recent MLA Job Information Lists (2004–2005) suggests that over 50 percent of all ads for composition and rhetoric specialists list administrative ability as either a required or desired qualification. Despite some of the problems associated with being an untenured administrator (e.g., difficulties negotiating departmental and university politics, inability to find time for research and writing required for promotion), many new PhDs in rhetoric and composition are hired right out of graduate school to direct writing centers, run first-year composition programs, or design Writing Across the Curriculum (WAC) programs. And even if newly hired composition and rhetoric faculty members are not expected to do administration right away, chances are very good that they will do it at some point in their careers.

If you are considering a nonacademic career track, keep in mind that you may also be asked at some point to take on a variety of tasks under the general heading of management: planning and organizing meetings, seminars, and special events; creating schedules and budgets; supervising the production and printing of written materials; and acting as a marketing, publicity, or writing director. Indeed, whatever the particular job, employers are always looking for the skills and abilities that would allow someone to take on administrative work. These include initiative (ability to propose and follow through with projects); organizational acumen; excellent communication skills; collegiality (you'll need to work with lots of different people); and leadership ability.

Formal Administrative Opportunities in Your Department

Administrative opportunities in graduate school can also be categorized in terms of their official status within a department or program. One of the most common formal administrative opportunities is an administrative assistantship. Administrative assistantships are awarded to talented graduate students (often those who have some graduate school and/or teaching experience) who possess the skills and abilities (mentioned above) required to help faculty administrators run their programs.

Instead of, or sometimes in addition to, teaching, administrative assistants help with such activities as

- New-TA or tutor orientation
- Faculty development (e.g., brown-bag discussions on teaching issues)
- Classroom/tutorial observations of TAs
- Visiting writer/lecturer series
- Program evaluation
- Department-sponsored scholarly conferences

The best graduate programs, recognizing the increasing demand for faculty-administrators, try to ensure that administrative assistants do as much meaningful administrative work as possible—not just busy work. Thus, it is becoming more and more common to see graduate students collaborating with faculty in the design of workshops and courses for new TAs, handling the major arrangements for visiting scholars, and codirecting conference events.

Another increasingly common way to get a taste of administrative work is through courses devoted to administrative concerns. More and more graduate programs are introducing "professional development" courses, which prepare students for jobs involving more than teaching and research. Students examine such issues as curriculum design, assessment methods, institutional and departmental politics, administrative ethics, and proposal- and report-writing strategies. Students also learn (through readings from journals that highlight administrative issues and requirements to subscribe to professional listservs[1]) how such work is theorized and researched, so they can join the growing number of scholars who publish articles and books on administrative efforts.

Because courses like these, as with many other formal administrative opportunities, often target rhetoric and composition students (because they are most likely to be hired as part- or full-time administrators), graduate students in other academic areas, such as literature or creative writing, may not think to enroll. Again, though, given the competitive job market in English studies, generally (particularly in literature and creative writing), and the fact that many faculty end up doing administration of some kind (if they aren't asked to do it initially), any opportunity to explore administrative work should be viewed as a chance to gain or develop expertise that will be attractive to employers and useful to you, whatever your area within English. In fact, it is not uncommon for talented graduate students in literature and creative writing who have course work or experience in rhetoric and composition to be hired to administer first-year writing programs and writing centers. And certainly administrative work of this type can lead to appointments as associate department chair, chair, or even dean—depending on a faculty member's interests and capabilities.

Formal Administrative Opportunities outside the Department

If your department doesn't offer assistantships or courses focused on administration, try looking outside of the department. Offices around campus often seek bright, energetic graduate students to hire, either through an assistantship or on a pay-per-hour basis. Such offices typically include those associated with the success of first-year undergraduate students. A Student Life or Student Affairs office, for example, will sometimes hire graduate students to help direct new-student orientation activities or design "college success" courses. Other good opportunities can be found in the many college or university centers that focus on a particular aspect of campus or community life (e.g., humanities centers, Jewish studies centers, women's centers, multicultural centers, international-student centers). If your teaching or research coincides with the work of a particular center, as it might if you are interested in diversity issues, for example, you will benefit even more from investigating administrative possibilities in this realm. Even if the work doesn't seem especially relevant, you will learn what academic culture is like and the range of jobs or careers possible within the academy. Those students who are considering nonacademic careers can benefit, too—not just from the practical experience but also from the opportunities to network with the local organizations and business leaders often associated with campus centers.

If you can see yourself as an upper-level academic administrator (e.g., dean, assistant vice president, vice president) at some point, it may also be worth your while to investigate whether your school has a program in higher education administration. Recognizing that top-level administrators benefit not only from the practical experience gained as program directors or department chairs, but also from concentrated study of the history of higher education, political issues, and organizational structures, more and more universities are offering course work and graduate-degree programs in these areas. Even if you don't wish to pursue an advanced degree in higher education administration, you may be able to take a relevant course to satisfy an elective requirement in your English program.

Informal Administrative Opportunities

If you are unable to get more formal administrative experience in graduate school, look for informal opportunities to develop these skills. These days, English departments, and programs within them, are busy with all sorts of initiatives that call for student volunteers. It may also be the case that some of the initiatives outlined under service above (e.g., conferences and speaker/lecturer series) will offer opportunities to plan or coordinate a special project. To get administrative skills, try to volunteer to chair a committee that will actually do something meaningful (e.g., supervise transportation and hotel accommodations for guests) rather than simply agree to make copies of flyers (that's more like service). Increasingly, assessment projects offer opportunities to get administrative experience. Though a faculty member will likely oversee a program evaluation, graduate students make welcome facilitator/organizers of small-group readings, data collection, and report writing. Again, as with service, you need to look for these opportunities, volunteer, and then shape them into an experience that will be useful.

Gaining Editing and Publishing Experience

Similar to administration, the necessity for developing editing and/or publishing credentials will depend upon the type of job you desire. In many English departments, professors are hired to edit scholarly journals, review manuscripts for literary reviews, or supervise student-run magazines. Even those who aren't hired for such work may eventually find themselves doing it.

Outside of academia, numerous career possibilities exist for people interested in editing and consulting. You might become a corporate writer and editor, producing newsletters, manuals, brochures, flyers, annual reports, company magazines, press releases, and even writing speeches for executives. Or you might become a technical writer or editor, producing technical publications such as letters, manuals, proposals, and press releases. Book publishers need editors and writers to review manuscripts, as you might imagine, but also copywriters and publicists. Newspapers, magazines, and advertising and public relations agencies need writers and editors of all sorts. The boom in electronic communications has opened up myriad jobs such as Web page master, software documentations writer, electronic game designer, not to mention CD-ROM editor, video editor, and others. Those of you whose specialty is creative writing might enjoy working as a fiction editor, play editor, romance novelist, or literary agent. Others of you may wish to become freelance writers and editors with clients in business and the academy, as well as private individuals who will pay for your services. Anywhere there is the written word, there is a need for writers and editors of all sorts—greeting card writers, medical writers, travel guide writers, dictionary editors—the list truly never ends.

Formal Editing Opportunities within Your Department

While you will pick up a certain degree of editing expertise through your courses (especially writing-intensive courses) and individual scholarly activities, you may benefit from more formal opportunities to review manuscripts and work closely with professional or aspiring authors. Aside from the text-review experiences mentioned in the service section, one of the most common ways to get formal editing experience is through an editing internship or assistantship. Such appointments are especially common in departments that sponsor professional journals. Faculty who edit journals in their disciplines are often eager to hire bright graduate students to review submissions for possible acceptance, communicate with authors, maintain data bases, solicit contributions, or to copyedit revised text.

Many fine literary journals (i.e., journals that publish mainly poetry, fiction, and essays) are run by undergraduate and graduate students, under the supervision of a faculty member, and these offer additional—and often more plentiful—opportunities to get this type of experience. Finally, more and more undergraduate programs are opting to design their own textbooks for introductory writing and literature courses. This can be a huge undertaking, involving sifting through mounds of already-published essays, stories, and poems; writing chapter introductions that reflect the department's interests and goals; and soliciting supplementary materials (e.g., syllabi, assignments, journal prompts) from faculty and TAs who teach the courses. Program directors welcome help from anyone who can make such a process run more smoothly and efficiently.

Formal Editing Opportunities outside Your Department

If an editing assistantship isn't available in your department, consider seeking out opportunities in other departments or in the local community. Always there are faculty or staff, trained in disciplines outside of English, who are working on any number of writing projects, from grants to research reports to professional journal articles. They often appreciate the insights that English graduate students can provide in such areas as organization, style, and usage. Some of these opportunities may even be paid. To keep abreast of opportunities across campus, ask a professor or graduate director to forward queries to you. These are often posted on university listservs. Your local community may also be a source of formal writing and/or editing experience. Nonprofit organizations, in particular, seek out volunteers who can help write grants, newsletters, and public-service announcements (PSAs).

Informal Editing Opportunities outside Your Department

If the more formal editing opportunities seem elusive, look for ways to gain this experience on your own. If your program or department doesn't have a newsletter, offer to start one. If you have technological expertise, volunteer to work on your program or department web pages. Another way that many graduate students get editing experience is to become involved in writing/research groups, which bring faculty and students together to share conference abstracts or article drafts-in-progress. Even if you feel strongly that your future professional life will not include editing—or the particular type of editing available in your department—you should consider the broader experiences that might be gained. Working with authors, facilitating revisions, and proofing final text can help you hone many of the communication, organizational, and problem-solving skills desired by employers. And, if you choose the academic route, such experiences will serve you well in your own writing and publishing.

Presenting Service, Administrative, and Editing Experience in the Job Search

As with your teaching and scholarship, you will want to keep track of everything you do in the areas of service, administration, and editing as you move along through your graduate program. Start by jotting down a list of all activities, committees, and assistantships that count in these areas. Then, make copies of position/assistantship descriptions and of the work samples you completed. Organize these in folders. Another good idea is to keep a journal or log, in which you summarize and reflect on your service, administration, and editing work—what you've done and what it has taught you. Such reflections will help you speak about your experiences throughout the job-search process.

Obviously, if a job announcement mentions any of these areas, you will want to discuss your experience in your application letter, highlighting, especially, the work that illustrates your suitability for the position. You will also want to be ready to *show* what you have done—to present examples of your editing work, for example, or descriptions of your service from peers and/or professors. One common method of demonstrating expertise in service, administration, or editing is to place samples of your best work in the dossier that your placement service will send to prospective employers.

Another option is to ask your recommenders to specifically talk about these areas in their letters. To help recommenders with this task, you will want to provide them with an outline of activities and sample materials. Finally, you should consider compiling a portfolio of work to present during interviews—especially if the position you are applying for emphasizes one of these areas. If the job announcement highlights administrative experience and abilities, for example, consider compiling an administrative portfolio that would include not only a list of administrative responsibilities you have had, but also documents you have designed or helped design, memos or reports you have written, titles of books you have read on administration, and evaluations from supervisors.

Note

1. Examples of such journals include *Academe*, which often publishes articles relevant to administrators across the disciplines; *Profession* and *ADE Bulletin*, which highlight concerns relevant to administrators of English departments; and *WPA:Writing Program Administration*, which, as its title suggests, focuses on issues related to writing-program administration.

Reference

Stygall, Gail. "At the Century's End: The Job Market in Rhetoric and Composition." *Rhetoric Review* 18.2 (Spring 2000): 375–389.

6 Survival Strategies for Graduate School and Beyond

Throughout this guide, we have suggested that the path to professional success begins with a clear sense of where you want to be after graduate school and ends with you landing the job you desire—or something close to it. Getting from A to B, however, isn't always simple. As you've already seen, there is much to consider as you are moving toward career goals: the published and tacit expectations of your program, ways to establish credentials in multiple areas, and how to connect experiences back to career goals. And there are many, often competing, demands. Most likely, your success will require a commitment to course work, scholarship, teaching and/or administration—but it will also require the ability to negotiate these various demands and the many accompanying anxieties.

In this chapter, we offer many strategies for coping with the demands of graduate school so that you will be more likely to succeed professionally

> Most likely, your success in graduate school will require a commitment to course work, scholarship, teaching and/or administration—but it will also require the ability to negotiate these various demands and the many accompanying anxieties.

and have more time and energy for personal needs, interests, and relationships. Though this chapter will be especially helpful to readers who are new to graduate school—or considering applying—much of the advice will apply to readers at all levels of experience.

The Multiple Stresses of Graduate School: An Overview

As we suggested at the beginning of this guide, graduate school can be a very stressful experience. This is especially true if you are in a competitive graduate program whose students are vying for a limited number of academic positions. In order to be a successful job applicant, you will not only need stellar grades and excellent references, but you will need to be able to demonstrate promise (if not excellence) in a variety of areas, including teaching, writing, and service. All of this can take an enormous toll—on your time, energy, and nerves.

The stresses begin in classes where reading and writing requirements are demanding and where active, insightful participation by all class members is expected. As we emphasized in Chapter 2, it is nearly impossible to skim theoretical articles and research reports the night before class and contribute meaningfully to a graduate seminar. Similarly, the writing you do will be gauged not only for its clarity and correctness (characteristics valued in undergraduate courses), but also for its depth, intelligence, and ability to contribute to larger, disciplinary conversations on key issues. Instead of cranking out papers a day or two before they are due (a practice not uncommon among undergraduates), you will find it necessary to start your work way in advance—sometimes months before a project deadline.

If you are fortunate enough to be awarded an assistantship, you will experience the added stress of learning how to balance your responsibilities as a student with your obligations as a teacher, researcher, administrator, or editor (depending on the kind of assistantship you secure). Though most assistantships are theoretically half-time (twenty hours per week), they often end up requiring more of your time—especially if the work is new or unfamiliar. Classroom teaching, for example, can be incredibly time-intensive when a teacher is first learning how to design course materials, organize interesting lesson plans, facilitate discussions, and respond to student work. Such stresses increase, of course, for those students who have responsibilities beyond school, such as child care, parent care, community service, or outside employment. Here, the ability to multitask becomes crucial, as does the capacity for moving in and out of various roles, some of which will seem at odds with each other.

Perhaps one of the biggest stresses of graduate school is financial. Unless you have substantial savings, are supported by a parent or partner, or have incredibly meager needs, you will feel the monetary pinch that almost always comes with student status. Though most assistantships include tuition reimbursement and a stipend, the reimbursement is often partial and may exclude student fees; the average stipend is $8,000–$12,000 per year, which is not enough for most people to live on. If you take out a low-interest loan, as many students do, you may feel pressure to complete your studies quickly, before too much debt accrues. A related concern is health benefits—something few graduate students receive, even though many are employees of universities through assistantship programs. Graduate students who do not receive health benefits usually must rely on catastrophic university-student health plans that offer affordable premiums, but carry high deductibles and pay-per-service costs. These plans typically work well for very healthy students (who don't actually need to use them).

Finally, all of the most obvious stresses of graduate school can contribute to other stresses—at home, at work, and among friends. Because studying for classes or fulfilling obligations for assistantships requires so much time and attention, you may find that there is precious little left of you for anything else. Parents, partners, children, and friends may start to feel neglected which, in turn, may make you feel guilty, adding yet another stress. Such is especially the case for women graduate students, who still, on average, are expected to do more care giving and relationship tending than their male counterparts. (See more on gender issues at the end of this chapter.) If you are in a dual-income relationship, and you give up your job to return to school, the changed financial circumstances may cause some tension in your relationship, too.

Surviving the Stresses: A Few Proven Strategies

As you embark on—or continue with—your graduate studies, you may want to consider that the most successful students aren't always the most certifiably brilliant. Instead, they are often the students who, though quite "book smart," are especially good at setting and prioritizing goals, focusing on the task at hand, organizing their time, sticking to schedules, and maintaining a positive outlook. Such aptitudes are required to meet deadlines and finish programs. They also help to reduce stress levels, by allowing a sense of control over circumstances that may seem complex at best, and chaotic at worst. Finally, these strategies make it possible for students to reserve time and energy for personal interests and issues.

> The most successful students . . . are especially good at:
> - setting and prioritizing goals
> - focusing on the task at hand
> - organizing their time
> - sticking to schedules
> - maintaining a positive outlook

Setting and Prioritizing Goals

> Some days it feels as if an angry pack of the flying monkeys from *The Wizard of Oz* has swooped into my classroom, my office, and my apartment and upended everything. Students want feedback to their drafts. Teachers want thesis essays, annotated bibliographies, and revisions to critical essays. Sometimes, friends actually want me to leave my apartment to go somewhere other than campus. No matter how much I try to plan, there's always a lecture or a reading to attend, or another story to read and line-edit for a workshop. During my most stressful times, I've contemplated running away to join the circus, because I'm sure I could juggle better than any other clown. (Gerrity 135)

Among the qualities that distinguish successful new professionals from those who struggle—in any field—is the ability to set and prioritize realistic goals. Graduate school, because of its multiple demands, offers a great opportunity to develop this ability. Because there are many professional-success guides available that offer good suggestions for setting and reaching job-oriented goals, we will focus here on considerations that will be most relevant to you, as a graduate student.

Most popular advice guides will tell you that it's helpful to set large goals first, and then set small goals to help you reach the larger ones. As we've been suggesting throughout this guide, in the wider arena of professional development, it can be helpful to decide what type of career you want and then design a plan for building your credentials. If you seek a position at a research university, and your professors tell you that you will need at least two published articles to be competitive, you will want to set smaller goals for revising course papers into articles at least a year (ideally, two years) before you begin applying. That way, editors will have time to send your work out for review, get the reviews, and notify you of their decisions. If you know that the hiring team for your ideal position will be looking for a variety of teaching experiences, you will need to start thinking about how you will teach different courses—or in different contexts—during graduate school. One smaller step toward this end would be to determine that you will teach two different classes by the end of your third term of graduate school, and then to add at least one more, if possible, by the time you finish your second year. Some graduate programs, as part of their mentoring efforts, will offer new graduate students examples of two- or five-year plans (depending on the degree) for short- and long-term goal setting. Figure 6.1 provides an example from the University of Nevada-Reno.[1]

In terms of more specific aspects of graduate school, you will also need to practice goal setting—with an eye toward your larger employment objective. As we suggested in Chapter 2, you will want to determine way in advance which courses you need to take, when they are offered, and how you will satisfy these requirements as efficiently as possible. For individual classes, you will need to be able to identify the major requirements (usually those that are the largest percent of the course grade) and plan the small steps needed for completing them successfully. Most graduate seminars require a research project, for example, that counts for anywhere from 25–40 percent of the course grade. Early in the semester, you will want to determine (with your professor, if necessary) what the expectations are, in terms of depth and breadth of research, level of analysis, and format. (Some professors talk about these matters in class; some do not.) If you know you will need to read thirty-five books on your topic, you will want to set goals for obtaining the books, reading them, and taking notes. And you will want to make sure your reading and note-taking goals are met far in advance of any writing deadlines. Dividing up the work into manageable segments, or smaller goals, will allay the stress and help you complete a better project.

Of course, to set realistic goals (i.e., goals that you can actually achieve in the time allowed), you will need to have a clear sense of how much reading, writing, class preparation, etc., you can accomplish, in a set amount of time, when you're at your best (i.e., well rested and alert). If you are just starting graduate school, this will take some practice— and time, time to become familiar enough with the new demands to gauge your capabilities. If, as a new graduate student, you don't have

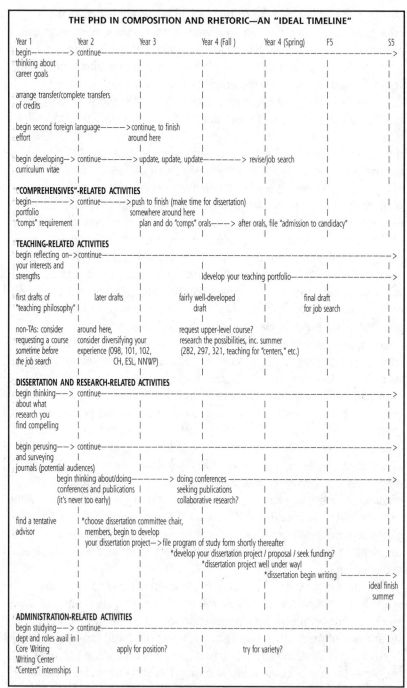

Figure 6.1. Sample PhD timeline.

much experience analyzing theoretical articles, you may need more time for reading and writing response papers, for example, than you will during your second semester of study. If you have an assistantship, you may also be unfamiliar enough with the work that it will take you longer to complete at first. New teaching assistants nearly always find that they spend much more time planning classes, preparing lectures, and/or responding to papers during their first semester of teaching than in subsequent semesters. So, while it may be unrealistic for a new teacher to set Friday afternoon as her goal for reading and responding to forty essay drafts received on Wednesday morning, a seasoned teacher may be able to achieve the goal fairly easily.

> To set realistic goals (i.e., goals that you can actually achieve in the time allowed), you will need to have a clear sense of how much reading, writing, class preparation, etc., you can accomplish, in a set amount of time, when you're at your best.

Finally, it's hard to achieve the goals you set for yourself if you have trouble prioritizing them. Because you will have goals in many areas—not just scholarship or teaching—you will need to decide which goals are most important or, more accurately, when certain goals should take precedence over others. It can be helpful to see time in terms of "investment." Given your larger objectives, and more immediate goals, where should you invest your time, and how much time do you need to invest to get the return you desire? If, for example, you are going on the job market next year, it will make more sense to invest your time in activities that will help you get a job, rather than in those that won't. That is, if you are hoping for a full-time faculty position at a research-oriented university and have a choice between revising a well-received conference paper for publication and helping a graduate student in mathematics with her writing, you should probably spend the time on your own writing. (You can always return to tutoring after you complete the article.)

> It's hard to achieve the goals you set for yourself if you have trouble prioritizing them. Because you will have goals in many areas— not just scholarship or teaching—you will need to decide which goals are most important or, more accurately, when certain goals should take precedence over others.

One of the most common struggles that new graduate students experience is determining what's most important.

A typical dilemma involves that of a new graduate student who has been awarded a teaching assistantship. She knows that she has to put most of her time into her courses in order to learn as much as possible and get high grades, but she also knows that effective teaching requires an enormous amount of time. The tendency is for new students to tip the balance toward their teaching because (1) others (students, program directors) are depending on them to do a good job; (2) teaching-related work needs to be done now, while studies can wait until something major is due; (3) teaching is often more fun than studying. The problem with this logic is twofold: studies usually can't wait for reasons we mentioned above; and if you don't do well in your courses, your teaching assistantship probably won't be renewed. In short, the students who are depending on you won't have you at all.

Setting priorities is also important when you look at the smaller picture. Take a particular course, for example. It is very common for students to feel they need to put all of their effort into every requirement. Such an approach is only realistic if you are taking two courses, at most, and have no other obligations. Most successful students will determine right away which requirements they need to dedicate more time and energy to, and which they can successfully complete with less effort. The grade breakdown that appears on most syllabi will be one indication. For example, if informal reading responses are 10 percent of the grade, and a theoretical presentation is 25 percent of the grade, then you know that you should put more time and thought into the latter requirement. Sometimes, though, you will need to ask your professor what her pedagogical priorities are—and what the specific expectations are for various requirements (if not spelled out on the syllabus). Both of us have had experiences with students who spend hours and hours preparing perfectly polished five-page weekly reading responses, when we were expecting shorter, more informal papers.

Managing Time

Related to goal setting is managing the time needed to reach the goals. Most successful professionals will tell you that the best time-management approach is to make a list of what needs to be done and then divide it into categories according to due dates: what needs to be done now, what needs to be done within a few days, within a month, etc. Then, it's a good idea to write up a schedule and stick to it. If a paper needs to be done in a week, consider first how long that project will likely take you to complete and then determine how many hours over the next week you will need to devote to it. If you think it will take seven hours to complete—and you have seven hours—great. If you only have five hours, you will need to be as efficient with your time as possible, which will involve your goal-setting skills again. At this point, break the project into five segments that might be realistically completed in an hour each. You might decide, for example, to write one page by the end of each hour or to divide the time in terms of your writing process, allowing two hours to draft, two hours to revise, and one hour to edit. Again, the important element in this is sticking to the schedule.

Those who struggle with time management often have many competing responsibilities; yet, they also may have some unproductive attitudes or habits. One common misconception is that big blocks of time are absolutely necessary for getting work done. Very few modern students can regularly devote big blocks of time to studying, writing, or class preparation. If you can set aside such time, consider yourself lucky. If you can't, try to make efficient use of the time you do have. For instance, while you may not be able to carve out three or four hours each day for your academic work, you may be able to set aside a few hours once or twice a week. Scholar John Goldsmith describes this approach in *The Chicago Guide to Your Academic Career*: "I like to teach in the morning, keeping at least a couple of afternoons each week clear to come home and work on my research" (Goldsmith, Komlos, and Gold 185). We would add that, besides any afternoons you can set aside regularly, make use of smaller blocks of time—even forty spare minutes here or there. Though you may not be able to get much polished writing done in a single forty-minute session, you can brainstorm a list of ideas for future drafting, revise a paragraph or two, or proofread a section. Routinely taking advantage of smaller blocks of time will keep you progressing and, most important, help maintain your momentum. In fact, in his research on scholarly productivity, Robert Boice found that compared to their colleagues who did their writing in sporadic "binges," "writers who work on a schedule of brief, daily sessions not only produce more manuscripts but also prose that is judged as more fluent and creative" (23, 25). And smaller time segments are perfect for designing a teaching lesson or responding to student papers. In fact, many instructors find that spreading out their paper grading over, say, a week (e.g., five papers per day) has many advantages over evaluating twenty-five papers in one long session. It minimizes reader burnout and,

> One common misconception is that big blocks of time are absolutely necessary for getting work done. Very few modern students can regularly devote big blocks of time to studying, writing, or class preparation. . . . Routinely taking advantage of smaller blocks of time will keep you progressing and, most important, help maintain your momentum.

as graduate-TA Maggie Gerrity suggests, increases the likelihood that each paper will be read "with the same open mind and good attitude" (137).

Another bad habit is to be too generous with the time you give yourself, taking, essentially, as much time as you can without toppling over from exhaustion. A good maxim here is that you will use up as much time as you allot yourself. That is, if you tell yourself that you need ten hours to complete a project, you'll take the ten hours, even if you might have been able to do it perfectly well in five.

"The Two P's"

Two of the biggest time-management issues for graduate students might be termed "the two P's." These are *procrastination* and *perfectionism*. Both habits can be time and energy wasters, and both create unnecessary stress. Procrastination typically means "putting off until tomorrow what can be done today." The problem with procrastinating in graduate school is that you simply won't be able to complete quality work if you wait until the last minute to do it. Of course, some amount of putting off work might actually be productive. For example, writers often take walks or showers between drafts in order to let their subconsciousness deal with a topic—or to gain some critical distance from a text. To understand whether you are taking productive pauses or simply putting things off, try keeping a journal of your work habits and consider how they do (or don't) help you complete projects successfully.

Nearly as debilitating as procrastination is perfectionism. This occurs when you try to make every response, every paper, every instructional lesson perfect. The problem with perfectionism is that even if you could be perfect (and you can't), you would be spending more time than you need to, and probably more time than you have. A good rule of thumb for graduate school is to learn what is "good enough" for the goal you have in mind. If you desire an A on a paper, for example, you could spend twenty-five hours on it, or twenty hours on it and still get an A, depending on how prepared you are, how efficient, and how clearly you understand the expectations. That is, the five hours spent on perfectionism might feel productive, but might not actually lead to any appreciable difference in the product.

> A good rule of thumb for graduate school is to learn what is "good enough" for the goal you have in mind.

Finally, graduate school provides a good chance to learn how to protect your time— not just from your own unproductive habits but from outside influences. It can be tempting to say "yes" to every invitation to join a committee, collaborate on a project, or socialize. Yet, if you are already very busy, you will want to accept invitations judiciously. Our advice is to say "yes" to activities that will clearly help you professionally—either because they support your career goals or will help you maintain the relationships, perspective, and sense of humor necessary to survive graduate school. Try to learn to say "no" to activities that feel draining, rather than productive and exhilarating. Honing this skill will be invaluable to you later in your career, when demands on your time will be even more overwhelming.

Staying Organized

Of course, all of the goal-setting and time-management advice offered above will mean little if you are unorganized. At the very least, you will need a good calendar to keep track of due dates and meetings. You will also save time, in the long run, by maintaining a list of frequently used phone numbers and e-mail addresses. Most e-mail programs have directories for storing such information, but you may not have access to your computer every time you wish to contact someone. An old-fashioned address book or day-timer can be carried with your billfold in a purse or book bag. The new handheld computers, which combine calendar, address book, and computer, are also a good option.

In the Work Space

The continuing emphasis on texts in English graduate programs offers another organizational challenge. It is easy to become overwhelmed by stacks of library books, texts for courses you are taking and teaching, copies of research articles, drafts of course papers, and piles of student homework. If you haven't already done so, now is the time to develop a system for organizing all of this material. First, you will want to create your own work space at home and at school. Your work space should include, at minimum, a desk, bookcase, and file cabinet. (If space is an

issue at school, you may have to settle for half of a shared desk, a
bookshelf, and a file drawer.)

- In your desk drawer(s), you might store the office supplies that
  you use regularly: pens, pencils, stapler, staples, manila folders,
  envelopes, and other items.

- With respect to your bookcase(s), you will want to develop a way
  to help you find the books you need quickly. Our advice is to
  categorize your books into distinct sections, based on the purposes they serve (e.g., books for classes you are taking, books for
  classes you are teaching, books for thesis research, etc.). Within
  these broad categories, and depending on how many books you
  have, you might categorize further—by author or topic, for
  example.

- Now is also a good time to develop a filing system. Most
  professionals will tell you that the key to a good filing system is
  that it makes sense to you—and helps you find things easily.
  Filing options include categorizing by topic, by author, genre, or
  by time period (e.g., Renaissance)—or a combination of these. If
  you have one or more filing cabinets, you might consider
  dedicating a drawer to each aspect of your developing professional life, e.g., course work, scholarly projects, teaching, etc.

On the Computer

Additionally, because you will be doing much of your work on a
computer, you will want to develop ways of organizing your computer
files. You might devote a disk to each aspect of your work—or to each
term, whatever makes most sense to you. Also, it will be important, in
terms of efficiency and stress-level, to always remember to back up the
work you do on your computer. For work that you can't easily replace or
re-do, back up three times: once on a disk, once on a hard-drive, and
once in printed paper form.

Making Connections

E. M. Forster's mantra "Only connect" can be a helpful guide for
graduate students. Making connections among courses, between various
roles and responsibilities, and with others can be crucial for surviving
and succeeding in graduate school.

Connecting Courses

Establishing connections among courses, for example, can help you save time. Instead of seeing each course, and each course project, separately, try to identify where and how they overlap—and whether this overlap can be tied to your personal and professional interests. If you are taking courses in modern British literature and modern rhetorical theory, for instance, you might identify overlap in the larger disciplinary move from seeing textual meaning as stable and definitive to seeing it as more fluid and indeterminate. In fact, you might be able to draw comparisons between the literary view and the rhetorical view of a modernist writer like Virginia Woolf. Assuming that a research project is a requirement for both courses, you would do well to see if you could write papers on the same general topic, using many of the same sources—but with different focuses, purposes, and audiences.

Connecting Selves

Identifying and drawing connections among your various roles or "selves" can also work to minimize the sense of fragmentation, and related stress, that often accompany advanced study. On the one hand, for example, you are a student and, as such, will tend to give professors and administrators extra respect and authority. On the other hand, you may be a teacher within your program, which provides you a certain degree of institutional power (especially among your students) and positions you as a colleague of the faculty members you admire. As we mentioned earlier in our guide, many professors regard graduate students as apprentices—as neither simply students nor peers, really, but something in between. To further highlight the complexities of the situation, your professors may treat you more like a student when you are in their classes, but more like a colleague when they see you in the halls or at departmental social events. If you are a parent, or if you have a job outside of the graduate program (particularly, if you are a full-time professional), your graduate-school identity will seem even more multifaceted—indeed, it may seem schizophrenic. Consider the mental shifts required to write a smart-sounding reading response in the morning, teach a first-year writing class at noon, go over your child's homework after school, and work on the books for your free-lance consulting business in the evening. While this may seem an extreme example, the scenario is becoming more and more common, especially as mature adults feel freer to change career paths and return to school.

The tendency is to see our many roles as separate, but they needn't be perceived that way. In fact, there are numerous areas of potential overlap. For example, taking on a student identity for your graduate seminars can actually help you be a better teacher. You can examine your own successes and struggles for insights into how you might assist your students. If you have workplace experience, consider how that might inform your classroom teaching. Could you share some of your business-writing experience with students in a composition class? Are you able to give students in your literature class some real-world tips on making good presentations? If you are a parent, think about all of the similarities between motivating students to succeed and inspiring your children to meet expectations.

Connecting Personally

Your success and satisfaction as a graduate student will also likely rest on your ability to establish or maintain connections with others—within and outside your department or program. From a practical standpoint, you will need people with whom to vent frustrations and celebrate successes—especially if your family, closest friends, or partners know very little about academic work. From a professional perspective, the relationships you build in graduate school often become an important support network throughout your career. Many professors begin career-long research and writing relationships with friends and professors they first met in graduate school.

> Relationships you build in graduate school often become an important support network throughout your career.

Of course, as with many aspects of professional life, building relationships can sometimes be very tricky. First, it can be hard to find quality time to spend on relationship building. The best advice we have, emphasized again below, is to schedule time for this activity. Consider the more routine moments of your day (e.g., lunch, coffee break, study break) and see if they can be shared with a colleague (who also needs to do these things). Another difficulty with relationships is that sometimes it takes time to figure out not only which peers you might enjoy being with, but also whether they are discrete. Expressing frustrations is something we can only do comfortably with people we trust. There can be much at stake for you if your private remarks are shared with others, especially if those remarks include grumblings about difficult classes or professors (the same professors who will be reading your exams, approving your thesis, and writing letters of recommendation).

Finally, you will want to be aware of the sometimes hazy line between personal and professional relationships and how crossing it can lead to confusion and disappointment. This is especially true with relationships between students and professors. It is quite common in graduate school for students and faculty to develop professional friendships. After all, many graduate students are the same age as their professors, and they often share a deep commitment and passion for particular authors, topics, and issues. Though these relationships may sometimes feel personal, they should not be regarded in the same way as your other close relationships. As long as you are a student (i.e., until you have earned your degree), any relationship with a professor will be imbued with very real differences in power and authority—in ways that social friendships typically are not. You will especially want to avoid any relationship with a professor that could be construed as romantic. While romances between professors and students do sometimes occur, they are viewed as highly unethical (because of the obvious power differential). In fact, professors can get fired for "fraternizing"—and universities can get sued. Our best advice is to steer clear of any ties with faculty that could be interpreted as anything other than professional.

Collaborating with Others

One way to maintain a sense of connectedness with others is to collaborate. On a very basic level, collaboration might involve simply brainstorming seminar-paper ideas with classmates or studying for comprehensive exams with other students who have finished their course work. A very common form of collaboration, especially among creative writers, is a "writers' group"—something we discuss in Chapter 4. Here, students and/or faculty meet regularly to share work in progress and get feedback from other writers. A less-common, but very important, type of collaboration involves coauthorship, where people with similar interests conduct research and write together—often creating a single text.

The benefits of collaboration are numerous. Obviously, collaboration helps minimize feelings of isolation. Also, because professional collaborations often include discussions of work conditions, office politics, and even personal issues, they can provide opportunities for venting frustrations and achieving new—and often more balanced—perspectives. Collaborations also offer an alternative to the more traditional, competitive relationships that advanced study sometimes inspires. For all of these reasons, collaboration can alleviate many of the stresses of graduate school. From a practical standpoint, collaborations can help you set and keep deadlines. Since others are involved, you know you aren't the only one who pays a price if you miss a deadline, and that can be a real motivator. Finally, collaboration during the researching, writing, and studying process often leads to a better product. Most people who collaborate regularly feel that the diverse perspectives gained through collaboration ensure a richer result—and, perhaps just as important, a more enjoyable process.

> Most people who collaborate regularly feel that the diverse perspectives gained through collaboration ensure a richer result—and, perhaps just as important, a more enjoyable process.

Of course, as with any activity, collaboration has its potential pitfalls. The best collaborations are those that involve people who can speak openly and frankly to one another—especially when they disagree—and have complementary work styles. Sometimes, though, the only way to find people with whom you can productively collaborate is through the kind of trial-and-error process that includes some bad experiences. Both of us, for example, have collaborated with people whose communication styles and writing processes were so different from ours that it was difficult to get work done at all, let alone end up with a product we felt good about. Such collaborations can be especially challenging if there are differences in professional status or authority (as is the case when professors and students collaborate on projects). If you find yourself in a collaborative process that is not working, you will want to weigh the benefits of sticking it out (e.g., publication, grant money, etc.) against the drawbacks (e.g., unfinished work, hurt feelings). You will also want to remember that even bad experiences can be good learning opportunities. If you take the time to analyze uncomfortable collaborations, they can help you identify and assess your own strengths and weaknesses as a partner or group member (so that you will be better prepared to find a good collaborative match next time). At the very least, they will help you appreciate the good experiences when you find them.

Maintaining Personal Relationships

While we have emphasized professional success throughout this guide, we recognize that it is just one dimension of a fulfilling life. Most of us need to focus time and attention away from work toward personal relationships with friends and family, developing hobbies and outside interests, and just reflecting. In fact, rather than taking away from professional life, as it may sometimes feel, attending to the personal realm can actually enrich professional possibilities, giving us more energy for work projects, more perspective, and more patience with others.

Making Time

Of course, the most obvious obstacle to attending to the personal realm during graduate school is the feeling that there is no time for anything outside of school. Because it is true that it will be hard for you to *find* time in a busy schedule for personal interests and relationships, we suggest that you get into the habit of *making* time. To make time, you will need to prioritize friends, family—and yourself—regularly and pencil this commitment into your schedule first, before school responsibilities. And, as with school responsibilities, you will need to stick to the schedule. Sticking to the schedule will be easier if you make your personal commitments during days or weeks that you don't have major projects due or large stacks of papers to grade.

Another less-obvious way of making time for friends and family is to try not to see your professional life as separate from your personal life (something we suggest in this chapter's section on making connections). You can bring the two worlds together by talking with those who are closest to you about your schoolwork; showing them your papers, poems, teaching materials; and even inviting them to attend a conference or lecture with you. You might even find ways to collaborate with friends and family on scholarly or creative projects. If you are interested in issues of voice, or authority, among women writers, for example, you might not only research the published literature in that area, but interview your friend who works as a counselor at a woman's resource center.

Of course, it is easier to bring your professional and personal worlds together if your loved ones are interested in what you are doing and genuinely want to hear about it. You may find, though (as many people have), that friends and family grow resentful toward the teaching and studying that seem to be stealing you from them—especially if they are not academics themselves. During their time with you, the last thing they want to do is talk about school. If you find yourself in this situation, you will not only need to close your books and turn off the computer for a few hours; you will also need to suspend any school-related thinking as much as possible. Just tell your subconscious to work on that research issue or teaching problem that's been bothering you so that your conscious brain can devote its attention to more personal matters.

Learning How to Be Your Own Best Advocate

Your student status in graduate school may cause you to feel as if others (e.g., professors, graduate director, assistantship supervisor) will take care of you throughout your degree program. To some extent, this will be true. Most faculty members feel responsible for the well being of their students—in fact, some feel downright protective. This sense of responsibility, however, may not always translate into concrete moves that will help you finish your program. And, no matter how smart you are, no matter how many wonderful papers or stories you write, you usually cannot meet your career goals if you don't finish your degree.

As we have suggested throughout this guide, you will need to set goals and design an agenda to help you meet those goals. Because you are not working in isolation, however, you will also need to be firm with others along the way. If you plan to go on the job market next year, you need to sit down with your advisor and talk frankly about what you still need to do to get your degree and/or position yourself well for the job search. Ideally, the two of you will design a schedule for finishing that you both will agree to follow. Approaching your advisor and talking frankly about your goals will require you to be assertive—something that is often very difficult, especially if there is a large age difference between you and your advisor. It can help to remember that being assertive does not equate with being aggressive or arrogant. You can

> Approaching your advisor and talking frankly about your goals will require you to be assertive—something that is often very difficult. . . . It can help to remember that being assertive does not equate with being aggressive or arrogant.

approach the situation by acknowledging your professor's experience and asking for his or her perspective on how you can achieve your goals. You might start the conversation by saying, for example: "I've set next June as a deadline for completing my thesis. Because you have so much experience as an advisor, I'm hoping that you can help me design a schedule for completing my work by then."

Another way to advocate for yourself is to make sure that others in your program, especially faculty, know of your expertise and accomplishments. Remember, faculty are often in a position to recommend students for assistantships or special projects, and you want them to think of you when opportunities arise. Also, they will be serving as references for you, even if you seek nonacademic employment. You want them to be able to talk in detail about your potential and accomplishments. Many students resist publicizing their experiences and accomplishments because it may seem like bragging. Again, as with assertiveness, the way you approach the situation is key.

1. **First, look for natural opportunities to advocate.** If you are interested in, say, a departmental assistantship or internship, look for opportunities to speak about experiences that would make you a good candidate. A class discussion on teaching methods, for example, might be the time to mention your many years of experience as an employee-development manager for a local business. Such experience would make you a strong applicant for an assistantship involving new-TA mentoring.

2. **Look for promotional forums.** A program newsletter or department listserv might be the perfect place to announce special accomplishments during graduate school (e.g., papers accepted at conferences, publications, awards). A personal achievement can easily be framed as a benefit for the whole program or department. You might begin your announcement with the larger benefit in mind, as seen in the following sample e-mail:

> Dear Professor Smith:
> Because the next issue of the program newsletter is coming out soon, I wanted to let you know that my paper was accepted for the upcoming modern literature conference. I think other students have received acceptance notices, too. Publicizing these student successes might encourage the dean to allot more money for graduate-student conference travel.

3. **Keep your health and general sanity among your priorities.** This may be the best way to advocate for yourself. If you fall ill due to stress, or have a mental breakdown, you obviously will have trouble meeting your goals. Again, because it will be hard to find time to exercise and relax, you will probably need to make time. Try to pencil twenty to thirty minutes into your day

for such activities. Just as we suggested in early sections, you might look for opportunities to combine activities you need to do anyway (e.g., travel to work, take a lunch break) with exercise and relaxation. If you usually drive to school, but the campus is within walking distance, consider taking the extra time to walk. Or, if you must drive, park in a lot that is a good distance from your building and walk the rest of the way. Similarly, instead of taking thirty minutes to eat your lunch, try to eat your lunch in ten or fifteen minutes, and use the rest of the time to walk around the campus. For relaxation, use the "extra" time for recreational reading (i.e., no schoolbooks allowed!). Finally, don't discount the value of professional counseling. If you are feeling over-whelmed or depressed, you may just need an outside, objective—and experienced—person to highlight various possibilities for thinking about or reacting to the issues you are encountering in graduate school. Many universities offer counseling services to students (some focused specifically on graduate-school success) at a significantly reduced rate.

> Because it will be hard to find time to exercise and relax . . . you might look for opportunities to combine activities you need to do anyway (e.g., travel to work, take a lunch break) with exercise and relaxation.

Keeping Some Perspective

Remember those posters that show a wide-angle shot of the universe with a tiny speck to indicate where we (as in Earthlings) are? Well, you might want to keep that poster in mind during graduate school. It may seem at times that your program or department *is* the universe, especially when paper or exam deadlines loom. And, of course, much of the work you do—especially if you teach—is important to the well being of others. In the larger scheme, though, what you are doing, though important, is not crucial to the continued existence of the planet. In fact, what you need to acknowledge is that your work isn't even crucial to the continued existence of your program. To be sure, graduate students help universities teach larger numbers of students with smaller amounts of money, but students come and go, and because of this, your time in the department is, in the big picture, quite short (which is one reason why you will not want to get involved in department politics). Conversely, given that most people now live into their seventies and eighties, the two-to-six years you will spend in graduate school is a very small part of your life picture.

Even if you accept the idea that "school is short and life is long," as Peter Elbow has pointed out in debates about teaching writing, you may find it difficult to maintain this perspective—especially when you are struggling. As with life generally, it can be difficult to maintain perspective when you don't do as well as you hope—or even fail. It can help to acknowledge early on that failure is a necessary element of most success stories. It is very rare for anyone to achieve success without experiencing setbacks along the way. So, expect some failure. More importantly, learn how to deal with failure when it happens. If you get a B on a paper, and you expected an A, don't automatically accuse yourself of being unintelligent—or your professor for being too tough. Instead, assume the best of both of you. Use the situation as an opportunity to do a little research on why you earned the B and what you might have done differently to earn an A. Start by meeting with your professor to get his or her perspective. Try to find out who in the class earned As (your professor won't be able to tell you this) and ask if you can read their papers to see what you could do differently next time. If your school or department has a writing center, meet with a tutor (a graduate student, if possible) to get her or his perspective. That is, instead of acting defensively (as many of us do when we disappoint ourselves), try to move offensively, by establishing a plan to do better next time.

Another challenge to a healthy perspective is idealism. Many people who pursue graduate study imagine a scene where intelligent, insightful people gather in hallways and faculty lounges to engage in spirited conversations about the latest theory or National Book Award winner. They also often imagine academics to be above petty politics and office gossip, spending almost all of their time reading, writing, and reflecting on aesthetic issues. While you might see glimpses of this picture, you will also notice that, similar to other work environments, people devote much of their time to very mundane activities, such as reading and responding to student papers, designing lesson plans, grading quizzes, and reading what they have assigned for class the next day. Also, just like any other workplace, there will be politics. In fact, because of tight resources for higher education, academics can feel even more protective of their territories (scholarly areas, courses, programs) than employees in a nonacademic context. And such protectionism can lead to office battles over who gets what and why. Most faculty will be

careful not to involve students in departmental politics, but if you do
see or hear something unpleasant, it may be easy to become disillu-
sioned. Try to simply recognize office politics as a necessary aspect of
the working world—and one that isn't all bad. Almost all program
revisions, new courses, proposals for additional faculty, and improved
processes are the result of political negotiations.

Being a Professional

In Chapter 2, we covered many of the tacit expectations of graduate
school, including responsibility, autonomy, and collegiality. These
expectations, which fit under the general term *professionalism*, often
determine the survival and eventual success of graduate students, and
being aware of them can spare you much of the stress experienced by
graduate students who haven't yet learned the professional code. So, it
bears reiterating that students who act professionally often succeed
professionally. Acting professionally includes dressing appropriately;
interacting with peers, professors, and staff members in a productive,
respectful manner; avoiding office gossip; and honoring deadlines and
other commitments. It also means using appropriate methods for
addressing concerns or resolving complaints. For example, most professionals understand that the best method for solving a problem is to
address it locally (e.g., with the people who are directly involved). For
you, acting locally would mean taking a complaint about a course to
the professor first, and trying to resolve the issue with him or her,
before talking to the department chair. Even when you are experiencing
internal stresses of all sorts, always be sure to conduct yourself professionally.

Special Challenges Related to Diversity

Gender Issues

Throughout this chapter, we have tried very hard to provide general
advice that will seem relevant to readers, no matter what their field
within English, and no matter where they are in the process of working
toward a degree. Before we close, though, we need to acknowledge the
unique circumstances of students who, because of their gender, race,
ethnicity, nationality, age, class, and/or sexuality, have perhaps felt
alienated from many aspects of advanced study.

In reading the professional-development literature, speaking with
students and colleagues who identify themselves as members of histori-

cally marginalized groups, and considering our own academic experiences, we've come to see that the advice we have provided applies broadly, but that certain students will need to pay even more attention to it. If you are a woman, for example, you may find it more difficult to negotiate your personal and professional roles than your male peers—especially if you have (or wish to have) children. Though men, as a group, are now shouldering a greater share of domestic responsibilities, research continues to show that women still do more in this realm than men. This fact is substantiated in the academy by the growing number of conference presentations, articles, and book chapters, written by women scholars across the disciplines, on the difficulties of being an academic parent. With titles such as "Caught between Two Worlds: Mothers as Academics" and "Mothers in the Academy: Positioned and Positioning within Discourses of the 'Successful Academic' and the 'Good Mother,'" this scholarship shows that while women *can* do it all—while they *can* be both professors and mothers—they often require more time to do it: more time to complete their course work, more time to finish their dissertations, more time to meet expectations for promotion and tenure. And they require encouragement from professors and peers who may be reluctant to see domestic responsibilities as valid rationale for "stopping the tenure [or degree] clock." While more and more departments and universities are supporting academic mothers by providing course-load reductions, longer work leaves, and slower tracks toward tenure, there is still a tacit expectation that personal issues should not interfere with professional work. That said, academic women who publicly discuss the challenges often point out the many benefits of parenting to their professional careers. Leonard and Malina found, for example, that academic mothers "may be less wrought up about work, less bruised by the politics, less likely to sit about in rooms late at night agitating about who said what to whom. Quite simply, they haven't got the time" (36).

Along with working harder to negotiate the competing demands of home and school, women students may need to make more of an effort to figure out the hidden agenda(s) of graduate study. Research indicates that women (especially older, returning students) struggle to meet the tacit expectations of their professors much more so than men. Many of these expectations (e.g., taking the initiative, developing a sense of autonomy) are more familiar to male students because they have been encouraged to develop such skills and attitudes from a young age. Research also suggests that women may have to work harder to "play

> Many of the more tacit expectations of a graduate school program (e.g., taking the initiative, developing a sense of autonomy) are more familiar to male students because they have been encouraged to develop such skills and attitudes from a young age.

the game" once they understand it. Through their interviews of academic women, Aisenberg and Harrington noticed a tendency to "reject" processes or activities that seemed like political game playing. Women "rejected—or still reject—the idea that playing games to advance themselves is necessary. They believed—and still want to believe—that people advance in the academic profession primarily through merit" (52).

Racial, Ethnic, and Class Identities

Like women, students of color sometimes find the tacit expectations of graduate school perplexing—especially when those expectations are based primarily on beliefs typical of white culture. The literature on graduate-student mentoring suggests, for example, that minority students may struggle with such issues as how to approach people with higher status (e.g., professors) with questions or problems, how to disagree with professors and peers, and, for students from "collectivist cultures," how to achieve individual success without minimizing the efforts of others (Davidson and Foster-Johnson 558). Though less has been written about social class as a factor in professional development, many scholars who identify their economic backgrounds as "poor" or "working class" also describe feeling alienated by the culture of academia, which, according to Fay and Tokarczyk, "barely acknowledges working-class existence" (3). These scholars, often the first in their families to attend college let alone pursue graduate study—report having only a vague, if not wholly inaccurate, vision of academic reality. As Donna Langston writes in "Who Am I Now? The Politics of Class Identity,"

> Most academics from working-class backgrounds end up on the bottom of the academic heap. They receive little guidance or mentoring from professors, which is particularly detrimental because their network of family and friends is not connected to academia. They are expected to know instinctively how to do all the things that one does in that world. Access to education and to decent jobs is based on inherited advantage. If one has no familiar-

ity with academic models of professionalism, she is at a great disadvantage. (68)

Discourse Conventions and Identity

Another aspect of graduate school that poses special challenges for some students is academic discourse. Numerous studies have shown, for example, that women often struggle with the writing conventions privileged in academia—conventions that reflect a masculine academic tradition. As Gesa Kirsch points out, though all students "struggle with the production and reception of academic discourse," women "have a different point of departure than men: they first have to establish a place of authority before they can begin to speak and write with confidence" (20). Establishing such authority, Kirsch goes on to say, often requires breaking the unspoken rules: using narrative when formal argument is expected, referring to self when detachment is the norm (19–22). Unfortunately, these breeches in convention are not often viewed positively—as necessary steps for acclimation to a new environment, or interesting innovations that will help expand our definition of acceptable writing. Instead, according to Kirsch and others, they are too often seen as evidence of ineptness or inability.

In addition to gender, racial identity can influence facility with traditional academic discourse forms. Numerous minority scholars, male and female alike, have written about their struggles to communicate ideas and insights in ways that mainstream (mostly white) academic readers would find acceptable. Comparing her dissertation-writing process as an African American to the second-language-learning process of one of her ESL students, Sheila Carter-Tod writes, for example:

> What could I say to her when my experiences with standard academic English had been so similar? Had I not seen the forms of expression that had been shaped by my family stories, and my readings of storytellers, be put in their "nonstandard" place? Had I not watched my own work be edited by others "for better form," feeling the life revised out of my own writing "for coherence"? Did I not watch, with frustration and helplessness, as my committee imposed what seemed like *its* form and organizational patterns on *my* study? (140)

Similarly, because academic discourse reflects middle-class values—as well as white, male points of view—students from working-class backgrounds sometimes feel uncomfortable with traditional scholarly forms of writing. Even those whose writing skills are praised by professors often describe feeling torn between an allegiance to "home" literacy practices, which are often more oral, narrative, and communal, and their desire to succeed with school practices that privilege print sources, objectivity, and individuality. In "Writing and Teaching with Class," fiction writer Valerie Miner describes her own move from a working-class environment, where "there were few books in our house," to the academy as "an immigration" to "a country where a different language is spoken." As she explains it, a career focused on writing is "particularly alien" to working-class students "because it embraces literacy, sometimes the major obstacle to parents' success" (77).

Teaching and Identity

Social factors can influence early teaching experiences, too. Recent collections of teaching narratives by graduate students (some of which are listed in Appendix A) highlight unique challenges for teaching assistants who are female (especially if they are young); identify themselves (or can be easily identified by others) as members of minority groups; are nonnative speakers of English; and/or are openly gay or lesbian. Though economic background is often more invisible, it, too, can play a role in terms of confidence-level. Langston, for example, depicts the discomfort she felt about meeting middle-class expectations for social interactions and professional dress during graduate school (67).

Unfortunately, as Langston suggests in the extended quote provided earlier (see pages 114–15), and as we suggested in previous chapters, the consequences for violating the expectations of graduate school—or of not quickly overcoming unique challenges—can be devastating. They include missed teaching or research opportunities (because faculty recommend the best students for special projects); poor grades; subpar teaching evaluations; and even dismissal. Perhaps more common are the less-obvious consequences—the self-doubt and subsequent drop in confidence that can come from negative school experiences. Because the consequences can be so serious, it is especially important for students from historically marginalized groups to both recognize the possible cultural sources of their struggles (which can be especially difficult if they identify as members of multiple groups, e.g., female, Mexican American, and working class) and to seek out good mentoring. Building support networks with students and faculty from similar backgrounds is crucial. Yet, because historically marginalized groups are still often underrepresented in academic departments, doing so may prove challenging. Minority faculty, for instance, are still relatively scarce. Because of their scarcity, those who may be on the faculty roster often find themselves burdened with committee service (especially service related to diversity issues) and advising of minority students. So, minority students, especially, must seek connections outside of their departments—and even outside their universities. Good options for establishing supportive external connections include:

- Conferences and listservs
- Campus groups and organizations devoted to addressing diversity issues
- Articles and books that provide practical professional-development advice for graduate students and faculty from diverse backgrounds (Many of these are listed in Appendix A.)

If you are a member of an historically marginalized group, you may also want to find ways to bring your professional and personal lives together by, for example, conducting research and/or writing on diversity issues. Informing professors and peers about your struggles as a woman or minority-group member can also be helpful, but trickier, too, as it might be seen as an attempt to get special treatment. One idea is to offer to organize a workshop on diversity issues or to speak to new TAs about how they might address diversity in their writing or literature courses. In this way, you will be highlighting the issues that concern you without making it seem that you are asking for favors. You also may find that in raising a particular diversity issue, you have moved your program or department along in the direction of greater awareness—especially if there is some type of follow-up to the event (e.g., subsequent forums, proposed policy or procedure changes, etc.).

Of course, sometimes the challenges faced by students from diverse backgrounds are the result of deliberate and inappropriate behavior of others and, thus, cannot be easily resolved through hard work and supportive mentoring. Such is the case with overt discrimination and harassment. If you feel that you have been discriminated against or harassed because of your gender, race, sexuality, physical ability (or any other status protected by law), you will want to familiarize yourself with your university's policies on discrimination and harassment, as well as its procedures for filing a complaint. Often, offensive behavior can be successfully addressed with a simple one-to-one discussion with the offender. If, after such a discussion, the behavior continues—or if you feel too intimidated to talk with the person by whom you feel harassed—you will want to take the appropriate, university-sanctioned steps toward resolving the problem. Your university's Human Resources or Affirmative Action website will give you the names and numbers you need to start the process.

Note

1. This chart was developed at the University of Nevada, Reno, by the faculty in rhetoric and composition (Kathy Boardman, Jane Detweiler, Christine Norris, Stephen Tchudi, Susan Tchudi, and Mark Waldo). It is a "situation-specific" revised version of a timeline Detweiler received from Brenda Jo Brueggemann while they were in graduate school together.

References

Aisenberg, Nadya, and Mona Harrington. *Women of Academe: Outsiders in the Sacred Grove.* Amherst: U Massachusetts P, 1998.

Boice, Robert. "Strategies for Enhancing Scholarly Productivity." *Writing and Publishing for Academic Authors.* Ed. Joseph M. Moxley and Todd Taylor. Lanham, MD: UP of America, 1992. 15–32.

Carter-Tod, Sheila L. "'In Search of My 'Jingle': Reconciling Voice and Identity After the Dissertation Defense." *The Dissertation and the Discipline: Reinventing Composition Studies.* Ed. Nancy Welch, Catherine Latterell, Cindy Moore, and Sheila Carter-Tod. Portsmouth, NH: Heinemann Boynton/Cook, 2002. 137–46.

Davidson, Martin N., and Lynn Foster-Johnson. "Mentoring in the Preparation of Graduate Researchers of Color. " *Review of Educational Research* 71.4 (2001): 549–74.

Fay, Elizabeth A., and Michelle M. Tokarczyk. "Introduction." Tokarczyk and Fay, 3–24.

Gerrity, Maggie. "Finding the Twenty-fifth Hour." *Finding Our Way: A Writing Teacher's Sourcebook.* Ed. Wendy Bishop and Deborah Coxwell Teague. Boston: Houghton Mifflin, 2005. 135–40.

Goldsmith, John A., John Komlos, and Penny Schine Gold. *The Chicago Guide to Your Academic Career: A Portable Mentor for Scholars from Graduate School through Tenure.* Chicago: U of Chicago P, 2001.

Kirsch, Gesa E. *Women Writing the Academy: Audience, Authority, and Transformation.* Carbondale: Southern Illinois UP, 1993.

Langston, Donna. "Who Am I Now? The Politics of Class Identity." Tokarczyk and Fay, 60–72.

Leonard, Pauline, and Danusia Malina. "Caught between Two Worlds: Mothers as Academics." *Changing the Subject: Women in Higher Education.* Ed. Sue

Davies, Cathy Lubelska, Jocey Quinn. Bristol, PA: Taylor and Francis, 1994. 29–41.

Miner, Valerie. "Writing and Teaching with Class." Tokarczyk and Fay, 73–86.

Tokarczyk, Michelle M., and Elizabeth A. Fay. *Working Class Women in the Academy: Laborers in the Knowledge Factory*. Amherst: U of Massachusetts P, 1993.

Appendix A: Chapter Resources

Chapter 1: Determining Your Professional Goals

It's difficult to set professional goals without first understanding the range of career options you will have after graduate school. Even within the realm of postsecondary teaching, possibilities abound—in terms of subject area, type of institution, and job responsibilities. Beyond the ivory tower, possibilities are even more numerous and varied. The following sources supplement our first chapter by providing more specific information about the kinds of professional positions that exist (both within academia and in the private sector); the likelihood of landing the position that most interests you (given today's job-market realities); and how to locate a graduate program that will best help you meet your employment goals.

Bay, Libby. "Teaching in the Community College: Rerouting a Career." *ADE Bulletin* 114 (1996): 27–29.

Bérubé, Michael. *The Employment of English: Theory, Jobs, and the Future of Literary Studies.* New York: New York UP, 1998.

Bly, Robert. *Careers for Writers and Others Who Have a Way with Words.* Lincolnwood, IL: VGM Career Horizons, 1996.

Dalbey, Marcia A. "What Is a Comprehensive University, and Do I Want to Work There?" *ADE Bulletin* 111 (Fall 1995): 14–16.

DeGalan, Julie, and Stephen Lambert. *Great Jobs for English Majors*. Lincolnwood, IL: VGM Career Horizons, 1995.

Donohue, Stacey. "What a Long, Strange Trip It's Been: Becoming a Community College Professor." *ADE Bulletin* 126 (Fall 2000): 42–45.

Dorwick, Keith, Dene Grigar, John F. Barber, Tari Fanderclai, Karen Howell, and Linda Jorn. "Looking Elsewhere: Career Options Other Than the Tenure-Track Teaching Position for M.A.s and Ph.D.s in English." *Computers and Composition* 17.1 (2000): 69–95.

Fenza, D. W., ed. *The AWP Official Guide to Writing Programs*. 11th ed. Paradise, CA: Dustbooks, 1999.

Gleckner, Robert F. "A Taxonomy of Colleges and Universities." *The Academic's Handbook*. Ed. A. Leigh Daneef and Craufurd D. Goodwin. Durham, NC: Duke UP, 1998. 3–16.

Grant, Daniel. "What Becomes of an MFA?" *Chronicle of Higher Education* 26 February, 1999. 4 November 2002 < http://www.chronicle.com/jobs/v45/126/4526sptlt3.htm >.

Howard, Carol. "The Transition from Graduate School at a Research University to Teaching at a Small College." *ADE Bulletin* 125 (Spring 2000): 37–39.

Krannich, Ronald L. *Educator's Guide to Alternative Jobs and Careers*. Woodbridge, VA: Impact, 1991.

Lim, Shirley Geok-lin. "The Strangeness of Creative Writing: An Institutional Inquiry." *Pedagogy* 3.2 (2003): 151–69.

McCormick, Kathleen. "Pedagogical Possibilities: The Needs and Benefits of Working at Teaching-Oriented Institutions." *ADE Bulletin* 133 (Winter 2003): 50–56.

MLA Committee on Academic Freedom and Professional Rights and Responsibilities. "Advice to Graduate Students: From Application to Career." *ADE Bulletin* 132 (Fall 2002): 49–53.

MLA Committee on Community Colleges. "Considering Community Colleges: Advice to Graduate Students and Job Seekers." *Profession 2003*. New York: Modern Language Association, 2003. 164–72.

MLA Committee on Professional Employment. *Evaluating the Mission, Size, and Composition of Your Doctoral Programs: A Guide*. New York: Modern Language Association, 1997.

Montel, Gabriela. "The Job Market for Creative Writing Faculty." *Chronicle of Higher Education*, 26 February 1999. 4 November 2002 < http://www.chronicle.com/jobs/v45/is6/4526splti.htm >.

Papp, James. "Gleaning in Academe: Personal Decisions for Adjuncts and Graduate Students." *College English* 64.6 (July 2002): 696–709.

Phelan, James. *Beyond the Tenure Track: Fifteen Months in the Life of an English Professor*. Columbus: Ohio State UP, 1991.

Smith, Hope. "Working in Publishing." AWP Web site. < http://www.awpwriter.org/careers/hsmith01.htm.

Stolpa, Jennifer M. "Settling for a Great Job." *Profession 2001*. New York: Modern Language Association, 2001. 85–91.

Vesilind, P. Aarne. *So You Want to Be a Professor? A Handbook for Graduate Students*. Thousand Oaks, CA: Sage, 2000.

Chapter 2: Making the Most of Graduate School

While intelligence, hard work, and excellent writing skills got you into graduate school, they likely won't be enough, by themselves, to ensure that you successfully complete your program and get the job you really want. As with most professional situations, the people who distinguish themselves are not just "book smart" and motivated; they are good at figuring out what is expected of them, when it's expected, and how to get it done. They are also adept at interacting with a variety of people (supervisors, professors, peers) in a variety of situations. The resources listed below offer both practical advice and personal testimony to help you understand the complex (and often hidden) expectations of graduate school and how to effectively meet these expectations.

Ervin, Elizabeth. "Power, Frustration, and 'Fierce Negotiation' in Mentoring Relationships: Four Women Tell Their Stories." *Women's Studies* 24 (1995): 447–81.

Fennelly, Beth Ann. "Things MFAs Are Expected to Know but Aren't Taught—and How Knowing Them Might Get You a Job." *AWP Job List* (August 2003): 1 & 14–15.

Goldsmith, John A., John Komlos, and Penny Schine Gold. *The Chicago Guide to Your Academic Career: A Portable Mentor for Scholars from Graduate School through Tenure*. Chicago: U of Chicago P, 2001.

Hawley, Peggy. *Being Bright Is Not Enough: The Unwritten Rules of Doctoral Study*. 2nd ed. Springfield, IL: Charles C. Thomas, 2003.

Peters, Robert L. *Getting What You Came For: The Smart Student's Guide to Earning a Master's or PhD*. Rev. Ed. New York: Noonday, 1997.

Preparing Future Faculty Homepage. < www.preparing –faculty.org > .

Sternberg, David. *How to Complete and Survive a Doctoral Dissertation*. New York: St. Martin's, 1981.

Welch, Nancy, Catherine G. Latterell, Cindy Moore, and Sheila Carter-Tod, eds. *The Dissertation and the Discipline: Reinventing Composition Studies*. CrossCurrents Series. Portsmouth, NH: Boynton/Cook, 2002.

Chapter 3: Establishing Yourself as a Teacher

For most graduate students, teaching is an intellectually rewarding—but definitely daunting—activity. There's always more to learn, more new techniques to perfect, more varieties of students to encounter, more theoretical questions to ponder, and more facets of English studies in which to develop teaching expertise. The materials we picked here cover the gamut of teaching—literature, composition, creative and nonfiction writing, English as a Second Language, writing across the disciplines, and tutoring in a writing center.

Anderson, Chris, ed. *Literary Nonfiction: Theory, Criticism, Pedagogy*. Carbondale: Southern Illinois UP, 1989.

Bernays, Anne, and Pamela Painter. *What If? Writing Exercises for Fiction Writers*. New York: Longman, 2004.

Bishop, Wendy. *The Subject Is Writing: Essays by Teachers and Students*. 3rd ed. Portsmouth, NH: Boynton/Cook, 2003.

———. *Working Words: The Process of Creative Writing*. Mountain View, CA: Mayfield, 1992.

Bishop, Wendy, and Deborah Coxwell Teague, eds. *Finding Our Way: A Writing Teacher's Sourcebook*. Boston: Houghton Mifflin, 2005.

Blau, Sheridan. *The Literature Workshop: Teaching Texts and Their Readers*. Portsmouth, NH: Heinemann, 2003.

Corbett, Edward P. J., Nancy Myers, and Gary Tate. *The Writing Teacher's Sourcebook*. 4th ed. New York: Oxford UP, 2000.

Curzan, Ann, and Lisa Damour. *First Day to Final Grade: A Graduate Student's Guide to Teaching*. Ann Arbor: U of Michigan P, 2000.

Davis, Barbara Gross. *Tools for Teaching*. Higher and Adult Education Series. San Francisco: Jossey-Bass, 1993.

Diogenes, Marvin, and Clyde Moneyhun. *Crafting Fiction: In Theory, In Practice*. Mountain View, CA: Mayfield, 2001.

Enos, Theresa, ed. *A Sourcebook for Basic Writing Teachers*. New York: Random House, 1987.

Forche, Carolyn, and Philip Gerard, eds. *Writing Creative Nonfiction: Instruction and Insights from the Teachers of the Associated Writing Programs.* Cincinnati: Story Press, 2001.

Gillespie, Paula, and Neal Learner. *The Allyn and Bacon Guide to Peer Tutoring.* 2nd ed. New York: Pearson Longman, 2004.

Good, Tina Lavonne, and Leanne B. Warshauer, eds. *In Our Own Voice: Graduate Students Teach Writing.* Boston: Allyn and Bacon, 2000.

Graves, Richard L., ed. *Rhetoric and Composition: A Sourcebook for Teachers and Writers.* 3rd ed. Portsmouth, NH: Boynton/Cook, 1990.

Haake, Katharine. *What Our Speech Disrupts: Feminism and Creative Writing Studies.* Urbana, IL: National Council of Teachers of English, 2000.

Hedengren, Beth Finch. *A TA's Guide to Teaching Writing in All Disciplines.* Boston: Bedford/St. Martin's, 2004.

Jacobus, Lee A. *Teaching Literature: A Collection of Essays on Theory and Practice.* Upper Saddle River, NH: Prentice Hall, 1996.

Lightbown, Patsy, and Nina Spada. *How Languages Are Learned.* Oxford, UK: Oxford UP, 1993.

Lindemann, Erika. *A Rhetoric for Writing Teachers.* 4th ed. New York: Oxford UP, 2001.

McCormick, Kathleen, Gary Waller, and Linda Flower. *Reading Texts.* Lexington, MA: Heath, 1987.

McKeachie, Wilbert J. *Teaching Tips: Strategies, Research, and Theory for College and University Teachers.* 10th ed. Boston: Houghton Mifflin, 1999.

Mitchell, Rosamond, and Florence Myles. *Second Language Learning Theories.* London: Arnold, 1998.

Moore, Cindy, and Peggy O'Neill, eds. *Practice in Context: Situating the Work of Writing Teachers.* Urbana, IL: National Council of Teachers of English, 2002.

Moxley, Joseph M., ed. *Creative Writing in America: Theory and Pedagogy.* Urbana, IL: National Council of Teachers of English, 1989.

Reid, Joy M. *Teaching ESL Writing.* Englewood Cliffs, NJ: Regents/Prentice Hall, 1993.

———. *Understanding Learning Styles in the Second Language Classroom.* Upper Saddle River, NJ: Prentice Hall Regents, 1998.

Sadoff, Dianne F., and William E. Cain. *Teaching Contemporary Theory to Undergraduates.* New York: Modern Language Association, 1994.

Showalter, Elaine. *Teaching Literature.* Malden, MA: Blackwell, 2003.

Silva, Tony J., and Paul Kei Matsuda, eds. *On Second Language Writing.* Mahwah, NJ: Lawrence Erlbaum, 2001.

Slevin, James F., and Art Young, eds. *Critical Theory and the Teaching of Literature.* Urbana, IL: National Council of Teachers of English, 1996.

Tate, Gary, Ann Rupiper, and Kurt Schick, eds. *A Guide to Composition Pedagogies.* New York: Oxford UP, 2001.

Wilhoit, Stephen W. *The Allyn and Bacon Teaching Assistant's Handbook: A Guide for Graduate Instructors of Writing and Literature.* New York: Longman, 2003.

Yancey, Kathleen Blake. *Teaching Literature as Reflective Practice.* Urbana, IL: National Council of Teachers of English, 2004.

Young, Art, and Toby Fulwiler, eds. *When Writing Teachers Teach Literature.* Portsmouth, NH: Boynton/Cook, 1995.

Chapter 4: Establishing Yourself as a Scholar

It's helpful to see the scholarly work you do in grad school as being part of a continuum extending into professional life, whether as a professor or independent writer. The pieces we've selected here include manuals and guidelines to publishing in different English subfields, tips for scholarly productivity, and specific advice on scholarship issues likely to confront you throughout the stages of grad school (such as writing your first grant proposal or converting seminar papers into conference presentations and theses into books).

Boice, Robert. "Strategies for Enhancing Scholarly Productivity." *Writing and Publishing for Academic Authors.* Ed. Joseph M. Moxley and Todd Taylor. Lanham, MD: UP of America, 1992. 15–32.

Boyer, Ernest. *Scholarship Reconsidered: Priorities of the Professoriate.* Princeton, NJ: Carnegie Foundation for the Advancement of Teaching, 1990.

Fulton, Len, ed. *The Directory of Poetry Publishers.* 20th ed. Paradise, CA: Dustbooks, 2004.

———, ed. *The Directory of Small Press/Magazine Editors.* 35th ed. Paradise, CA: Dustbooks, 2004.

———. *The International Directory of Little Magazines and Small Presses.* 40th ed. Paradise, CA: Dustbooks, 2004.

Gibaldi, Joseph. *MLA Style Manual and Guide to Scholarly Publishing.* 2nd ed. New York: Modern Language Association, 1998.

Harman, Eleanor, Ian Montagnes, Siobhan McMenemy, and Chris Bucci. *The Thesis and the Book: A Guide for First-Time Academic Authors.* 2nd ed. Toronto: U of Toronto P, 2003.

Henson, Kenneth T. *Writing for Publication: Road to Academic Advancement.* New York: Allyn and Bacon, 2004.

Holberg, Jennifer L. "Getting the Profession We Want, or A Few Thoughts on the Crisis in Scholarly Publishing." *Pedagogy* 4.1 (2004): 1–7.

"How to Get Published in ESOL and Applied Linguistics Serials." TESOL Web site. <www.tesol.org>.

Huff, Anne Sigismund. *Writing for Scholarly Publication.* Thousand Oaks, CA: Sage, 1999.

Locke, Lawrence F., Waneen Wyrick Spirduso, and Stephen J. Silverman. *Proposals That Work: A Guide for Planning Dissertation and Grant Proposals.* 4th ed. Thousand Oaks, CA: Sage, 1999.

Luey, Beth. *Handbook for Academic Authors.* 4th ed. Cambridge, UK: Cambridge UP, 2002.

———, ed. *Revising Your Dissertation: Advice from Leading Editors.* Berkeley, CA: U of California P, 2004.

MLA Committee on Academic Freedom and Professional Rights and Responsibilities. "Advice for Authors, Reviewers, Publishers, and Editors of Scholarly Books and Articles." *ADE Bulletin* 132 (Fall 2002): 107–11.

Nickerson, Eileen T. *The Dissertation Handbook: A Guide to Successful Dissertations.* 2nd ed. Dubuque, IA: Kendall/Hunt, 1993. (See especially sections on converting parts of dissertations into presentations.)

Olson, Gary A., and Todd W. Taylor, eds. *Publishing in Rhetoric and Composition.* Albany: SUNY P, 1997. (See especially chapters for graduate students.)

Ross, Donald, Jose Beruvides, and Pamela Behnen. "How to Write and Publish Articles on Literatures in English." <http://english.cla.umn.edu/faculty/ross/HowTo.HTM>.

Shinder, Jason, ed. *Get Your First Book Published and Make It a Success.* Franklin Lakes, NJ: Career Press, 2001.

U of Chicago P Staff. *The Chicago Manual of Style.* 15th ed. Chicago: U of Chicago P, 2003.

Chapter 5: Establishing Other Academic Selves

If you are considering a career that will allow you to pursue interests in service, administration, or editing/publishing, you should know that real-life experience will be your best teacher. That said, there are numerous articles and books on these aspects of professional life that can help you cope with issues or problems you may confront as a graduate-student committee representative, administrative assistant, or editorial intern; help you situate your experience within larger professional conversations; and help you confidently discuss your experience and abilities with prospective employers. Some of these are listed below.

Association of Writers and Writing Programs. *AWP Directors Handbook: A Compendium of Guidelines and Information for Directors of Creative Writing Programs*. Fairfax, VA: 2004.

Association of Professional Communication Consultants Homepage. < http://www.consultingsuccess.org>.

Brown, Stuart C., and Theresa Enos, eds. *The Writing Program Administrator's Resource: A Guide to Reflective Institutional Practice*. Mahwah, NJ: Lawrence Erlbaum, 2002.

George, Diana, ed. *Kitchen Cooks, Plate Twirlers & Troubadours: Writing Program Administrators Tell Their Stories*. Portsmouth, NH: Boynton/Cook, 1999.

Handstedt, Paul. "Service and the Life of the Small-School Academic." *Profession 2003*. New York: Modern Language Association, 2003. 76–84.

Harris, Jeanette G., and Joyce Kinkead, eds. *Writing Centers in Context: Twelve Case Studies*. Urbana, IL: National Council of Teachers of English, 1993.

Making Faculty Work Visible: Reinterpreting Professional Service, Teaching, and Research in the Fields of Language and Literature. Report of the MLA Commission on Professional Service. December 1996. < http://www.mla.org/ade/reports/index.htm>.

McLeod, Susan H., and Margot Soven, eds. *Writing Across the Curriculum: A Guide to Developing Programs*. Newbury Park, CA: Sage, 1992.

Murphy, Christina, and Joe Law, eds. *Landmark Essays on Writing Centers*. Davis, CA: Hermagoras Press, 1995.

Myers-Breslin, Linda, ed. *Administrative Problem-Solving for Writing Programs and Writing Centers: Scenarios in Effective Program Management*. Urbana, IL: National Council of Teachers of English, 1999.

Nelson, Jane V., and Kathy Evertz. *The Politics of Writing Centers*. Portsmouth, NH: Heinemann/Boynton-Cook, 2001.

Publishers Weekly Homepage. < http://publishersweekly.com>.

Rose, Shirley K., and Irwin Weiser, eds. *The Writing Program Administrator as Researcher: Inquiry in Action and Reflection*. Portsmouth, NH, Boynton/Cook, 1999.

Sharpe, Leslie T., and Irene Gunther. *Editing Fact and Fiction: A Concise Guide to Book Editing*. Cambridge, UK: Cambridge UP, 1994.

Silk, Bobbie Bayliss, ed. *The Writing Center Resource Manual*. Emmitsburg, MD: National Writing Centers Association P, 1998.

Society for Scholarly Publishing Homepage. < http://www.sspnet.org>.

Taylor, Rebecca G. "Preparing WPAs for the Small-College Context." *Composition Studies* 32.2 (Fall 2004): 53–73.

Walvoord, Barbara E. Fassler. *Helping Students Write Well: A Guide for Teachers in All Disciplines.* 2nd ed. New York: Modern Language Association, 1986.

Ward, Irene, and William J. Carpenter, eds. *The Allyn & Bacon Sourcebook for Writing Program Administrators.* New York: Addison Wesley, 2002.

Chapter 6: Survival Strategies for Graduate School and Beyond

The resources we list here are meant to supplement the more general bibliographies compiled for previous chapters by focusing specifically on issues often faced by graduate students and beginning assistant professors who identify themselves as members of historically disenfranchised groups. These sources include practical-advice guides, in-depth scholarly studies, collections of personal narratives, and short opinion pieces.

Benjamin, Lois. *Black Women in the Academy: Promises and Perils.* Gainsville: UP of Florida, 1997.

Bérubé, Michael. "Professors Can Be Parents, Too." *Chronicle of Higher Education* 48.31 (12 April 2002): B 12, 2p.

Bishop, Wendy, and Deborah Coxwell Teague. *Finding Our Way: A Writing Teacher's Sourcebook.* Boston: Houghton Mifflin, 2005.

Bonilla, James, Carlton Pickron, and Travis Tatum. "Peer Mentoring Among Graduate Students of Color: Expanding the Relationship." *New Directions for Teaching and Learning* 57 (Spring 1994): 101–13.

Bronstein, Phyllis, and Lori Farnsworth. "Gender Differences in Faculty Experiences of Interpersonal Climate and Processes for Advancement." *Research in Higher Education* 39.5 (1998): 557–85.

Caplan, Paula J. *Lifting a Ton of Feathers: A Woman's Guide to Surviving in the Academic World.* Toronto: U of Toronto P, 1993.

Coiner, Constance, and Diana Hume George. *The Family Track: Keeping Your Faculties While You Mentor, Nurture, Teach, and Serve.* Champaign: U of Illinois P, 1998.

Enos, Theresa. *Gender Roles and Faculty Lives in Rhetoric and Composition.* Carbondale: Southern Illinois UP, 1996.

Ferber, Marianne A., and Jane W. Loeb, eds. *Academic Couples: Problems and Promises.* Urbana: U of Illinois P, 1997.

Gray, Breda. "Women in Higher Education: 'What Are We Doing to Ourselves?'" *Changing the Subject: Women in Higher Education*. Ed. Sue Davies, Cathy Lubelska, and Josey Quinn. Bristol, PA: Taylor & Francis, 1994. 75–88.

Hong, Juli. "If I Had a Penis and a Mustache." Bishop and Teague, 76–83.

Lim, Shirley Geok-lin, and Maria Herrera-Sobek. *Power, Race, and Gender in Academe: Strangers in the Tower?* New York: Modern Language Association, 2000.

Looser, Devoney. "Advice for Academics Facing the Two-Body Problem." *ADE Bulletin* 134–35 (Spring–Fall 2003): 34–38.

Lynch, Kathryn. "An Immodest Proposal: Have Children in Graduate School." *Chronicle of Higher Education* 48.39 (7 June 2002): B5.

Melzer, Dan, and Paul Reifenheiser. "The Art of Academic Diplomacy: How to Finesse Departmental Politics as a Grad Student." Bishop and Teague 141–50.

Ostrow, Ellen. "An Academic Life out of Sync." *Chronicle of Higher Education* 49.38 (8 August 2003): sec. 3. C5.

Pascoe, Judith. "What to Expect When You're Expecting." *Profession 1994*. New York: Modern Language Association, 1994. 71–74.

Peterson, Susan. "Challenges for Black Women Faculty." *Initiatives* 53 (Spring 1990): 33–36.

Reese, Rita Mae, and Brandy T. Wilson. "We Teach Alone: The Lesbian Instructor in Academia's Lonely Groves." Bishop and Teague 102–7.

Sax, Linda J., Linda Serra Hagedorn, Marisol Arrendondo, and Frank A. Dicrisi III. "Faculty Research Productivity: Exploring the Role of Gender and Family-Related Factors." *Research in Higher Education* 43.4 (August 2002): 423–46.

Schneider, Allison. "Why Don't Women Publish as Much as Men?" *The Chronicle of Higher Education*, September 11, 1998. A14–16.

Szczepanski, Jay. "Reasonable Relationships: Gay Teachers and Straight Classrooms." Bishop and Teague 92–101.

Toth, Emily. *Ms. Mentor's Impeccable Advice for Women in Academia*. Philadelphia: U of Pennsylvania P, 1997.

Turner, Caroline Sotello Viernes, and Samuel L. Meyers, Jr. *Faculty of Color in Academe: Bittersweet Success*. Boston: Allyn and Bacon, 2000.

Appendix B: Overview of the Academic Job-Search Process

In many respects, your job search will begin the moment you enter graduate school—or, even before this, as you investigate programs and determine how they are aligned with your interests. If, early on, you follow the suggestions outlined in our initial chapters, you will think about the kind of position you want and how you can get the credentials you need to be a strong candidate. You will then begin (through course work, teaching, scholarly projects, and extracurricular activities) to more deliberately develop your professional credentials.

Toward the end of your program, you will start to think of the job search differently—less in terms of preparation (which has already happened) and more in terms of how to help prospective employers understand and appreciate your experiences and abilities. While many of you will pursue nonacademic positions, we focus here on the academic job-search process because it is similar enough to other search processes to make it generally relevant but different enough to warrant special, in-depth explanation.

Typically, the application process for an academic position involves most, if not all, of the following activities:

- Researching open positions through job lists mentioned in Chapter 1
- Preparing your dossier, including:
  - an academic vita
  - cover letters
  - letters of recommendation (from professors, supervisors, etc.)
  - current transcripts
  - samples of writing, teaching materials, administrative documents to showcase your strengths
- Submitting letters, vitae, and supplementary materials by published deadlines
- Providing follow-up materials if requested by an institution
- Scheduling interviews, if invited by an institution
- Preparing for different types of interviews (phone; convention; and, if you make the "final" cut, onsite)
- Considering job offers and negotiating contract details

Of course, these components may change, depending on the type of job, the particular subfield, and the timing of the initial position announcement. For example, search processes for tenure-track positions often differ from those for fixed-term or visiting positions. While initial personal interviews and subsequent campus visits are the norm for tenure-track jobs (especially those that are advertised early in the academic year), many applicants are hired for nontenure-track positions on the basis of phone interviews alone. Similarly, if an institution needs to fill a position in a subfield that is in high demand (technical writing is a good current example), it may forego initial convention or phone interviews and fly exceptional candidates directly to campus for an extended interview, after reviewing application materials and checking references. Finally, since some schools have to advertise positions late in the job-search season, because of last-minute budgetary approval or an unexpected resignation, they may not have time to conduct multiple interviews with candidates. So, like the institution mentioned above, they may simply collapse an extended review process into a single campus interview for two or three top candidates.

Because our guide is focused on the professional preparation that occurs before the job-search process, we cannot address all aspects of that process here. What we can offer are brief appendices that provide information and advice on three of the most important components of the job search: the letter of application; the teaching portfolio (which is increasingly requested by academic search committees either in part [e.g., the teaching philosophy statement and sample syllabi] or as a whole collection); and the interview. We have also included an appendix devoted solely to job-search resources that will both supplement our appendices and provide information on areas we have not covered in detail here (such as writing dissertation abstracts, drafting the vita, and negotiating job offers). As with all of your professional-development activities, we encourage you to start skimming the books and articles on this list as soon as possible so you will be well prepared when you submit your first applications for the academic position you desire.

Appendix B1: Tips for Writing Academic Job Application Letters

Cindy Moore and Glenn Davis, April 2004 (modified 7/18/05)

Many job applicants see the application (or cover) letter as a rather perfunctory part of the job-search process—as something routine, even formulaic. While, certainly, good letters conform to standard conventions (e.g., including date, recipient address, salutation, close), employers will tell you that the best letters demonstrate, through detail, the applicant's suitability for an advertised position, as well as an awareness of the employer's ongoing interests, current needs, and, to the extent possible, long-term goals. That is, successful application letters are not generic, one-size-fits-all efforts but are, instead, carefully tailored to meet particular audience needs and expectations. While the following suggestions are specifically designed for academic job applicants, most of them can be applied to the nonacademic job-search process as well.

Before You Draft Your Letter

Study the Position Announcement.

- What qualifications, abilities, and skills does it highlight?
- Are you qualified? How so?
- Can you talk about your experiences and credentials in a way that will convince a hiring committee/employer that you are a strong applicant?

Do Some Research. Check into the college, program, and/or department.

- What's the school's mission?

- What types of programs and courses does it offer?
- What are the typical credentials of faculty?
- What can the school's Web site tell you about its student population?
- Would you be a good fit? Why? If so, what can you do in your letter to emphasize this fit? (From a hiring-committee perspective, there is nothing more irritating than receiving a letter that emphasizes experiences and abilities that have little relevance to the publicized position, program, or institution.)

Take Stock of Unique Experiences.   Examine what you have that will make you a strong candidate for the position.

- Have you completed any course work in areas highlighted by the ad? If so, mention it.
- Do you have experience working with technology? Teaching diverse students (especially the type who attend the school you're interested in)? Again, be sure to highlight such experience in your letter if doing so will underscore your suitability for the position.
- Have you attended professional conferences? Served on university or departmental committees? Mentored new graduate assistants? Written in nonacademic contexts? If so, how can you frame this experience to match the position announcement or needs of the school?

Look at Sample Application Letters.   Most recently hired faculty or alumni will be happy to share their application materials with you.

- What do these letters have in common?
- How are they formatted?
- What do the introductions typically include?
- How are they organized? Look especially at how applicants talk about their teaching abilities, interests, experiences, and approaches.
- How do people discuss other aspects of their professional lives (e.g., research, professional development, service)?
- What's included in a typical conclusion?

Drafting Your Letter

Tailor Your Letter to the Job Ad.   Cover all of the areas highlighted in the ad, if possible. Use the research you conducted by referring to specifics of a school's mission, program, and curriculum. If you can, mention particular courses of theirs that you are qualified to teach. Remember that hiring committees want to know what you can do for them—not what they can do for you. So, avoid including self-interested statements like, "Because you offer graduate courses, I would be able to experience the joys of teaching at both the beginning and advanced levels."

Use Details.   Let your details show that you have the experience and skills that the school wants. For example, when you discuss your teaching background, don't just say that you have "taught various courses at different levels" or that you "use a student-centered approach"; show, through specific examples, what the breadth/depth of your experience is and what your approach looks like.

- What *is* your teaching philosophy—and how is this philosophy supported by your assignments, class activities, and instructional methods?
- What sets your approach apart from others?
- Are you innovative? How so?
- What do students, peers, and supervisors say about your teaching?
- What do you do in your classes that would help you teach the students at the school to which you're applying?

Two detailed sample passages, from different application letters, are shown in Example 1 and Example 2:

Example 1

My classroom experience has enabled me to work with a range of students, from those in their first semester of college to those completing advanced degrees. As an adjunct lecturer at _____, I designed and taught a graduate course on Old English language and literature. By the end of the course, the students were able to parse, translate, and explicate works of Old English prose and verse that were previously inaccessible to them; one student has since incorporated Old English poetry into her dissertation on the English epic. I have also taught nonmajor undergraduates at ____, both as a teaching assistant for surveys of British and American literature and as an instructor for two sections of Rhetoric and Composition. In all of these classes, I have tried to recreate the atmosphere of a small, liberal arts college at a large university by encouraging open dialogue and curiosity, as well as challenging rigid disciplinary boundaries. This goal was put to the test in the fall semester of 2000, when I taught a section of composition in the Gateway Program, which serves traditionally underrepresented students. I worked to help these students, the majority of whom were the first in their families to attend college, achieve not only a sense of academic independence but also an intellectual confidence that many of them lacked when they arrived at the university.

Example 2

My approach to undergraduate writing instruction has suited the variety of students I have encountered over the years. Typically, I use a writers' workshop approach, with students writing and revising regularly and receiving frequent feedback on their work from both me and small groups of peers. I emphasize connections between writing and reading by requiring a fair amount of reading, as well as informal textual analyses which ask students to think about what they might learn, as writers, from published texts. Additionally, my students facilitate discussions and give presentations on various writing issues—activities which reinforce the role of oral communication in the learning process. Because I use portfolio assessment, reflection and self-evaluation are important components of all of my undergraduate classes. The effectiveness of my teaching can be seen in consistently excellent evaluations from both students and faculty supervisors. I am especially pleased that nearly all of my students have noted in departmental evaluations that my classes have helped them improve as readers, writers, and critical thinkers.

Connect Your Research/Writing with Your Teaching. If there are many connections, consider devoting a short paragraph to these; if not so many, find ways to connect your thesis or dissertation project to your teaching experience or philosophy in teaching-oriented paragraph(s). Here is an excerpt from a letter that attempts to highlight research/teaching connections. After describing her feminist teaching approach, the applicant-writer of Example 3 discusses parts of her research project that reflect/inform her teaching.

Example 3

My interest in writing pedagogy has informed my research pursuits. For my dissertation, I conducted an ethnographic study of an advanced composition class in which students explored issues of voice, identity, and authority from a feminist perspective. Particularly important were assignments that invited students to break with academic conventions surrounding structure and style. Through a narrative account of the class, I highlight both the difficulties that can accompany moves away from such conventions and the benefits. In doing so, I address concerns raised by feminists and other critical theorists about the possible limits of traditional styles of analysis and argument, as well as claims made about the positive potential of alternative approaches.

Write Clearly and Concisely.   Remember that, for many positions, hiring committees will be reading hundreds of application letters. Letters which are difficult to follow, longer than necessary, and jargon-laden may end up in the "rejection pile," regardless of a candidate's qualifications. (Grammar, usage, or spelling errors are often "just cause" for immediate rejection.) Some good rules of thumb are to:

1. Organize a cover letter in terms of abilities or experiences stressed in the position announcement (e.g., if teaching seems a top priority for a particular school, discuss your teaching background early in the letter—perhaps immediately after establishing that you have met basic degree, dissertation, or course-work requirements).

2. Keep the letter to two pages, if possible (job ads that specify many different criteria or requirements may require a bit more).

3. Use enough academic lingo to show that you are informed but not so much that you turn off members of hiring committees who are not in your subfield. To ensure readability, use black ink on white stationery and a serif font style, such as Times New Roman, in 10 or 12 point.

After Your Letter Is Drafted

Get Feedback on Your Letter.   Show a draft of your letter to many people and try to get detailed responses. Though you will want to carefully consider all of the feedback you receive, realize that some responses may not be as helpful as others. Ultimately, your sense of purpose and audience—as well as your ideas about how to best represent your experiences and abilities—should determine which revision suggestions you will follow. After revising your letter, you may want to get some quick responses to the changes, too. Finally, if you are not a great proofreader of your own work (many good writers are not), ask one or two peers to proofread your revised letter (again, even one mechanical error can cost you an interview).

Prepare Your Letter. When you are satisfied with your letter, print it on high-quality department stationery (often called "letterhead")—and use high-quality black ink. Many departments will gladly give stationery to graduate students who are seeking employment; if a tight budget prevents this, offer to pay for the paper. Because first impressions often make or break a job search, this is not the time to be frugal.

Meet the Stated Deadline. Many schools will not consider applications received after a published deadline.

Include All Requested Materials. Review the job ad and refer to it as you gather materials for your application. Mention the materials toward the end of your letter (e.g., "As you requested, I have included my vita and names of three professional references."). Many ads will specify the number of reference letters that should be sent (commonly, three letters are requested) or the particular kinds of materials desired (e.g., a teaching philosophy and ten-page writing sample). Though it will be tempting to send more material than the ad requests, more isn't always better. Some hiring-committee members get annoyed when they are bombarded with unsolicited material. Others may unintentionally overlook the most important supporting information if it is buried within a stack of documents.

Appendix B2: Brief Guide to Compiling a Teaching Portfolio

As we suggest in Chapter 3, the teaching portfolio is an increasingly common way to demonstrate teaching effectiveness to hiring committees. In fact, recent nationwide calls for postsecondary teachers to document their teaching (for a range of purposes, including tenure and promotion, merit consideration, and program assessment) make it very likely that the teaching portfolio you compile for the job search will be the first of many such portfolios you will compile throughout your career. While not every position you apply for will require that you submit an entire portfolio, academic hiring committees routinely ask for materials that are typically included in portfolios—especially the statement of teaching philosophy, sample syllabi, and student evaluations. And even though a portfolio may not be requested, successful job candidates often bring their portfolios to interviews (especially on-campus interviews) in order to illustrate important points about their teaching experience and classroom strengths. Because the job-search process is usually very time consuming, you will want to prepare your portfolio in advance of sending out your first application letters. Doing so will allow you to focus on writing good letters as position announcements are posted and to quickly tailor your ready-made materials when hiring committees request them.

As with teaching generally, there is no one right way to compile a teaching portfolio. The most basic portfolio is simply a collection of teaching-related materials that depict a teacher's overall approach to instruction and his or her teaching experience. Most hiring committees, however, have come to expect more than a collection of sample syllabi and assignments. They want to understand a candidate's overall approach to teaching; the beliefs and values that inform the approach; how classroom practices detailed in syllabi and assignments reflect a candidate's scholarship and/or service interests; and whether a candidate's approach and practices are aligned with their departmental mission and/or program philosophy. For these reasons, highly effective teaching portfolios often include classroom materials as well as information that contextualizes those materials, such as a teaching philosophy, brief introductory notes, and teaching narratives.

What follows are some suggestions for compiling the kind of informative, integrated, persuasive portfolio that will help you get the teaching position you desire. The suggestions are meant to be read as a menu of sorts—a list from which you will pick and choose, depending on your goals. Following the lead of Peggy O'Neill, who has written specifically about job-search portfolios, we have divided our suggestions into four categories, which correspond with the writing-portfolio process often encouraged in composition and creative writing courses. The suggestions are based on the work of scholars like O'Neill, as well as our own observations and experiences reading and creating teaching portfolios.

Collaboration

The teaching portfolio is a perfect opportunity to practice what many of us preach as teachers. We encourage students to read and respond to each other's drafts in class, or to visit the writing center, but we often are reluctant to share our own work with peers and professors. As we implied in the "after drafting" section of Appendix B1, getting feedback on important job-search documents is crucial to your success. Your teaching-related materials are no exception. Ideally, you should work with one or two peers—and consult with a trusted professor—through the entire portfolio-construction process. As O'Neill points out in "Constructed Confessions: Creating a Teaching Self in the Job Search Portfolio," peers can help one another determine which experiences and talents to emphasize, how to talk about teaching strengths, and what materials to include. Further, because peers know you and, presumably, something about your teaching, they can help you "avoid self promo-tion and remain faithful to what [you] value and how [you teach]" (36). At the very least, you should ask one or two trusted peers to proofread everything, including your syllabi and assignment sheets. Again, errors in any written document can cost you an interview. (You are being considered for a position as an English instructor, after all.)

Another form of collaboration is to look at sample teaching portfo-lios and to get lots of advice on compiling them. Again, recently hired alumni or professors in your department are often excellent sources. You might also talk with professors who have served on hiring committees for searches that elicited teaching materials. In terms of published sources on teaching portfolios, one of the best we have found for job-search purposes is *Composition, Pedagogy, and the Scholarship of Teaching* by Deborah Minter and Amy Goodburn. Though only three chapters in this collection discuss job-search portfolios specifically (O'Neill's essay is one of them), all of them provide information and insights that can be applied to this particular type of teaching portfolio. The book also has a very useful companion Web site.

Collection

In Chapter 3, we advised you to begin saving samples of teaching materials early on in your graduate program so that you will have much to choose from as you start the job-search process. In the same chapter, we list the types of materials that are most commonly included in teaching portfolios (see pages 50–51). Other, less-common options include brief narratives about how particular assignments worked and a list (with brief descriptions) of graduate pedagogy courses you have taken (or workshops you have participated in) to prepare you to teach various courses. (Though graded student papers seem another logical option, some scholars advise against including them in the teaching portfolio because of risks related to reading papers out of the teaching and learning context [e.g., what you see as an A effort for a particular student, in a particular class, might seem a C effort—and evidence of laxity or grade inflation from another person's perspective]). Because you may want to demonstrate not only your ability to teach a range of courses but also your experience teaching in multiple contexts (if you have such experience), you will want to save syllabi, handouts, and student responses from any courses or workshops you conducted outside of your department—for the summer-orientation program, for example, or the writing center. Consider making an extra copy of everything you hand out to students (peers, faculty) and placing it in a single catch-all folder as you move along in your program. If you don't have much classroom teaching experience (perhaps you had a research fellowship during graduate school and were not required to teach; or, as a TA, you were only able to teach one type of course), you will want to develop sample syllabi for courses that your course work and/or thesis or dissertation research have prepared you to teach.

With respect to your final portfolio product, there are, again, no hard-set rules. It's helpful to create a master portfolio from which you can copy separate parts, as needed. This source portfolio might be contained in a sturdy three-ring binder. If you are asked (or decide on your own) to submit your entire portfolio to a search committee, you will want to make sure it's as light as possible. Plain, two-pocket folders in a color suggestive of professional work (e.g., black, blue, dark green—not hot pink) work well—especially for first-round interviews to which employers and candidates must travel great distances. (No one wants to haul around a bunch of three-ring binders.) Portfolio contents should be well organized and perhaps even prefaced with a table of contents or brief introduction that explains what you have included and why. The contents should be neat, clean, and printed in black ink on white paper (unless you want to use color to highlight a few key documents).

With respect to overall format, you will want to be aware that, increasingly, job candidates are making teaching materials available electronically by posting them on professional Web sites. These digital portfolios are an attractive alternative (for hiring committees and job seekers alike) because they are often easier than traditional portfolios for readers to navigate (especially if there are links for different aspects of a candidate's teaching background); they can be updated easily; and they help to conserve paper.

Selection

As you select materials to include in your teaching portfolio:

- You will want to think carefully about what you want your materials to say about you, as a teacher, and how they support your statement of teaching philosophy (discussed briefly in Chapter 3 and below).

- You will also want to consider the skills and abilities mentioned in the position announcements that interest you. It is quite common for job applicants to construct different portfolios for different types of jobs, drawing from the same accumulated source material. For a technical-writing faculty position, for example, you might want to include materials that demonstrate your familiarity with current conversations about document design. These same materials might not be as important to include in a portfolio geared toward a general-education litera-ture position.

- Finally, you will want to try to imagine how hiring committees will read the work you have included, that is, how they will "construct" you as a teacher and picture you in relation to their program.

Speaking from the hiring committee's perspective, Donna LeCourt depicts one possible "hidden agenda" for teaching portfolios:

> Looking for a clear "fit" with what we already do in our composition program is not what we are seeking in a tenure-track colleague. Rather, we hope to find candidates who are knowledgeable of recent scholarship in composition, can help us set directions for the program, and can institute curriculum for teaching assistants and non-tenure-track teachers that best meets our students' needs (102–3).

More than likely, such requirements were not specified in the advertise-ment for the position LeCourt had in mind. Fortunately, most hiring committees don't expect to see teaching portfolios until fairly late in the search process (e.g., during a personal interview), which allows some time to find out more about a department's unstated needs. After you have made an initial cut—especially if it means a personal interview—, you should feel free to ask the search-committee chair for information about departmental expectations and goals that might not be available on the department Web site.

Reflection

Compiling a good portfolio necessarily requires reflection as you consider what to include and why. This is the type of reflection that, while crucial, does not translate directly into actual portfolio documents. Yet, as part of this broader kind of reflection, you will be thinking seriously about what you do as a teacher and why you do it—and these considerations will form the basis of your philosophy-of-teaching statement, which is one of the most important documents in a teaching portfolio. It is also the portfolio document that is most often requested separately, sometimes as part of the initial application packet. Because the philosophy statement is so important, and because it will guide your overall selection process, we spend a bit more time discussing it than we do other elements of the portfolio.

As you may recall, Chapter 3 includes a sampling of questions that will help you start to develop a sense of who you are as a teacher—what your priorities are, what ideas have most influenced you, and how you reflect your priorities in your assignments, activities, and classroom methods. When you actually get to the point of writing your philosophy for the job search, you will need to make the move from self-evaluation to careful consideration of how readers will interpret the values and beliefs you highlight. In her extensive list of prewriting questions for drafting teaching statements, Ruth Mirtz includes several prompts intended to assist writers with the challenging task of representing themselves for a variety of audiences: "Who will read this statement and what do they value in teaching?" "Where do I disagree with colleagues (in department, school, discipline) and why?" "How does my teaching differ from (and share commonalities with) teaching in other departments and disciplines?" ("Teaching Statements" 52). While you will not want to simply say what you think others want to hear (which is nearly impossible anyway, given the diverse makeup of most hiring committees), you will want to be careful not to align yourself too rigidly with one approach or another. In the excerpt from Mirtz's job-search teaching statement below, you will notice that while she refers to specific theorists who have influenced her work, they represent diverse perspectives. Readers are likely to appreciate both her breadth of knowledge and her attempts to make connections between different ideas and approaches. Note, too, how Mirtz explicitly indicates her unwillingness to define her pedagogy too narrowly.

> The intellectual framework for my teaching philosophy is an amalgam of theories drawn from radical pedagogy, critical literacy, rhetoric, and research in learning from ethnographers and teacher-researchers. Paulo Freire, Henry Giroux, and bell hooks have been tremendous influences on the way I see power and resistance as forces to be managed in the classroom. Ann Berthoff, Peter Elbow, and other mainstream contemporary theorists have shown me how to focus on the workings of language to motivate and challenge students, although theorists such as M. M. Bakhtin and Lev Vygotsky have been even more helpful for defining the rationales and goals of my first-year composition courses. While I have not yet found a fully satisfying hypothesis for critical literacy which accounts for computer-networked communication, internet research, and student websites, I feel that area of study holds a great deal of promise for improving our instruction. Overall, however, none of these theories takes particular precedence over discovering for myself and with my students, through feedback and dialogue in the classroom, where my students are and where they need to go. ("Teaching Statement for Job Application")

As with your application letter and your portfolio, as a whole, you will want to try to tailor your philosophy for different types of positions. While you will not want to depict your core values and beliefs differently for different schools (you don't want a job at a school that doesn't respect your basic philosophy), you may need to cast discussions of your approach in various ways. For example, Mirtz's discussion, with its references to many high-power theorists and contemporary movements within rhetoric and composition may work best for a position in a research-oriented department, in which faculty are not only familiar with the terminology and scholars mentioned, but have read their work. The same paragraph might intimidate readers outside of the discipline who have kept up with pedagogical discussions in their fields, but who do not read much theory (or may even be resistant to the idea that theory is important). For these audiences, it might be a good idea to

drop the names and replace the more technical (and potentially intimidating) terms (e.g., "radical pedagogy" and "critical literacy") with other
more familiar or even more neutral terms (e.g., "student-centered,"
"critical thinking").

Importantly, as Mirtz, O'Neill, and other scholars demonstrate in
their published work on teaching portfolios, sustained reflection on
teaching not only leads to good portfolios and philosophical statements,
but it inspires self-understanding and personal growth. As O'Neill
comments, "[R]egardless of the ultimate purpose of the portfolio—or
the final portfolio product—the processes used to create it demand
reflection and theoretical engagement, which are necessary for growth
and development" (41). If you can, then, you will want to start these
processes as soon as possible, by keeping a teaching journal and talking
regularly with others as you move through your graduate program. For
most successful teachers, the reflection required for a teaching portfolio
is simply a more focused form of the thinking that they do daily, as they
plan lessons, determine student needs, and assess the effectiveness of
assignments and methods.

References

LeCourt, Donna. "Reading for Pedagogy: Negotiating the Complexities of
    Context from a Search Committee Chair's Perspective." Minter and
    Goodburn 101–9.

Minter, Deborah, and Amy M. Goodburn, eds. *Composition, Pedagogy, & the
    Scholarship of Teaching.* CrossCurrents Series. Portsmouth, NH: Heinemann,
    Boynton/Cook, 2002.

Mirtz, Ruth M. "Teaching Statements and Teaching Selves." Minter and
    Goodburn 43–53.

———. "Teaching Statement for Job Application Portfolio." Companion Web site
    for *Composition, Pedagogy, & the Scholarship of Teaching.* Ed. Deborah
    Minter and Amy M. Goodburn. 2002. May 2005. <http://
    www.heinemann.com/minter-goodburn>.

O'Neill, Peggy. "Constructed Confessions: Creating a Teaching Self in the Job
    Search Portfolio." Minter and Goodburn 33–42.

Appendix B3: Brief Guide to
Academic Interviewing

As with drafting effective application letters, preparing for successful
interviews involves some basic steps that don't vary much by type of

position. So, while we focus on academic interviews here, most of what we say will apply to those of you who have opted to seek nonacademic positions.

Types of Interviews

Phone

Because of recent budget crises across the country, colleges and universities are feeling additional pressure to cut costs. So, instead of interviewing at a national conference (which we discuss below), many hiring committees conduct preliminary interviews by phone—especially if the position is a nontenure-track one. If a school decides to interview you by phone, the department chair or, more typically, someone on the search committee will contact you to arrange a mutually convenient day and time. You will want to try to negotiate a time when you can be alone, at home or in your office, without distractions for the thirty to forty-five minutes typically required. You will also want to ask your contact person for the names of the people who will be interviewing you, so that, in addition to further researching the institution and the department, you can make sure to find out about interviewers' scholarly interests and teaching areas.

The upside to this form of interviewing is that everyone knows it is awkward. It's hard to talk to people when you can't see their facial expressions, and if multiple interviewers are using a speaker phone, the acoustics may be poor and distracting. Because of these obvious limitations, candidates typically get every benefit of the doubt. Also, if you are interviewed by phone, you can refer to notes and wear whatever is comfortable. At the same time, though, you will want to resist actually reading your notes (even phone interviewers can pick up on answers that sound too scripted), and you don't want to dress so comfortably (e.g., in pajamas) that you will have a hard time projecting professionalism.

Convention

Another common form of preliminary interview is the professional-convention interview—most notably the annual Modern Language Association (MLA) conference that occurs late in December. Depending on the type of position being filled, hiring committees invite a small number of promising candidates (usually five to fifteen) to interview with department administrators and/or search-committee members, in person, for 30–45 minutes. Invitations for MLA interviews are typically extended in late October through mid December (shortly after published application deadlines)—though it is not uncommon for candidates to be called right before the convention. When you are contacted by a school, expect the caller to ask if you are still interested in the position and, if you are, to negotiate a mutually convenient day and time for the interview. Typically, the caller will also tell you where the interview will take place (the usual venues are hotel suites or a convention-center auditorium with numerous interviewing tables). He or she will also give you either a hotel room number or a phone number, so you can contact the interview team, in case of emergency. (If the caller doesn't give you this information, ask for it.)

Planning for this particular type of interview is key to your success. Here are basic guidelines that you can supplement by reading some of the interview-focused sources in Appendix B4.

- Schedule interviews wisely. If you are lucky enough to get multiple interviews, try to spread them out throughout a day or over two days. Scheduling interviews back-to-back is not a good idea for two main reasons: 1) you will need time to relax and refresh your mind for the next interview and 2) if the interviews are in two different hotels, located far apart, you may have trouble making it to the second interview on time.

- First impressions count. Buy a couple of professional-looking (but comfortable) outfits if you don't already have them (these needn't be expensive). Most men wear dark suits with solid-color shirts and ties; most women wear skirt or pant suits, dresses, or a skirt with a professional-looking blouse, jacket, or sweater (depending on the weather).

- Prepare thoroughly, by anticipating questions, writing-out and rehearsing answers, and formulating your own questions (using suggestions under "preparation" below).

- Double-check interview sites (they sometimes change) when you arrive at the convention. You can do this by going to the Job-Information Booth at the convention center and asking a volunteer to confirm where particular schools are interviewing. If there is a discrepancy between what you were told when you were invited to interview—and what MLA has on record—call your school contact and verify the location.

- Arrive early. Try to be in the general vicinity of your interview (i.e., outside the conference hall or in the hotel lobby) fifteen minutes before your interview so you are not late.

- Get plenty of sleep the night before your interview(s). No amount of preparation can help you if you are too tired to think clearly. Consider packing a white-noise machine or ear plugs in case your hotel is located in a noisy area.

- Try not to let the strangeness of the interview situation bother you. If you are interviewed in a small hotel room (rather than a suite), don't be surprised if you are seated right next to a bed; in fact, don't be surprised if one of your interviewers actually sits on the bed! If you are interviewed in a large convention auditorium, try not to let people at nearby tables distract you. A good source of MLA stories that will help you put any strange experience in perspective is Emmerson's "When Do I Knock on the Hotel Room Door?" (See Appendix B4).

For jobs that are posted late in the year (e.g., after December 1), the MLA interview is not a realistic option. Some late interviews for rhetoric and composition specialists take place at the annual meeting of the Conference on College Composition and Communication (CCCC) in March. Similarly, creative writers are sometimes interviewed at the spring AWP convention. Other interviews occur either by phone or on campus later in the spring and even into the summer. This is why if you don't get an MLA interview, you shouldn't worry too much about your job prospects.

Onsite or "Campus"

At some point, either as the only interview or as a final interview, the school will bring you to campus to meet administrators, faculty, and students—and to get a feel for the campus and local environment. If you've made it this far, assume that the school is very interested in you. It is common practice for schools to either pay upfront for your travel expenses or to reimburse you, after the interview. Be prepared to answer the same types of interview questions, with individuals such as faculty members, the chair, and the dean, and, again, with groups of people such as department staff, hiring committee members, and graduate students. It is also common practice to ask candidates to teach a class or give a scholarly presentation. (You can consult professors and former graduate students for ideas about teaching presentations. For scholarly presentations, consult our section on delivering a conference paper for ideas; typically, your paper is drawn from your thesis or a seminar paper or longer piece of creative writing.) Usually, the person who contacts you about a campus interview will be very happy to tell you what your itinerary will be (schools often send an itinerary to candidates before the interview); how to think about the teaching demonstration (if required); and what to focus on in your scholarly presentation.

Again, preparation for the campus interview will be the key to your success. Here are some tips to make your onsite interviews go smoothly:

- Once you make travel arrangements, confirm who is picking you up at the airport if you are flying, where to park if you are driving, the name of your hotel and directions to it.

- Be prepared for long days filled with meetings and evenings filled with social events such as dinners and parties attended by members of the department.

- Be unfailingly gracious and professional to everyone from the school's janitor to the president; later everyone will be comparing notes about their impressions of the campus visitor.

- Don't let down your guard even at relaxing informal moments such as walking to the next event or socializing at a party. Campus visit legend has it that good jobs have been lost by campus visitors who drank too much or otherwise became indiscrete.

- Try to learn as much as you can about the prospective job to see if it is a good fit for you. It helps to take notes at the end of the day so that you can refer to them later when your memory is not as fresh.

- Generally, toward the end of your visit, the search committee chair or department chair will talk about specifics of the job such as teaching, research, and service/administration responsibilities, and the expected starting salary. If your schedule doesn't include a meeting with a human resources officer, the committee or department chair may also provide you with a packet that covers health benefits and retirement plans. All of this information is important because it will help you make a decision when you get an offer. However, this is not the time to negotiate the specific terms of employment; wait to see if the institution extends an offer first.

Preparing for Interviews

Anticipating Questions

If you have followed our advice up to this point, you will have the credentials and experience needed to answer basic questions about your teaching, scholarship, and service or administrative abilities and interests. Here are some examples:

- How do you teach composition/literature/creative writing?
- Describe your most successful assignment or activity (and/or your least successful).
- What are your strengths and weaknesses as a teacher?
- If I were to visit your classroom on any given day, what would I see?
- Describe your dissertation project.
- What were your responsibilities as an assistant director of the writing center/writing program/etc.

Most interviews, however, will require that you speak beyond *what* you did in graduate school to *how* and *why* you did it—and your particular goals for your professional future (especially if the position is "permanent," or tenure track). That is, in addition to a basic understanding of what a candidate has done in graduate school, hiring committees also want to know the theories and philosophies that have guided (or would guide) a candidate's teaching, scholarship, and/or administrative activities. Committees are also interested in the connections you see among the various facets of your academic life. With all of this in mind, you should be prepared to answer questions like these:

- What is your philosophy of teaching composition/literature/ creative writing?
- What theories (or theorists) are most important to you as a teacher of _____.
- What are the most important skills that English majors need to develop and why?
- How did you choose your dissertation topic/approach/methodology?
- How does your research contribute to the literature in your field?
- How does your research inform your teaching (or administration)?
- What is your five-year research plan?

- What is your philosophy of program administration?
- Why does administration interest you?

Finally, most hiring committees need to determine whether you will be a good fit for their department or program. So, in addition to the general questions listed above, prepare for more specific questions such as:

- How do you see yourself contributing to our program in ____?
- Why do you want a position in our department?
- What skills do you have that will allow you to successfully teach the kinds of students that enroll at the University of ____?
- What courses might we need to add to our literature/writing curriculum?
- How will your scholarship complement the scholarship of other faculty in our department/program?

To prepare for successfully answering interview questions, you will want to anticipate questions; conduct more research (e.g., by consulting school Web sites again); write out answers in advance; and get some feedback on your answers, preferably through mock interviews which involve professors acting as interviewers and then giving feedback on your answers.

Finessing Answers

Of course, you want to answer all questions as honestly as possible. Otherwise, you may find yourself in a position for which you are not prepared (and which could lead to termination, tenure denial, or even a courtroom). However, there are advantages to being careful about how you answer particular questions—especially questions that are geared toward determining where you stand theoretically or politically. Given that you will probably be asked about theory—and understanding (from Chapter 2) that many departmental tensions are rooted in theoretical disagreements—you will be smart to not pigeonhole yourself or your work too much. For example, though you may be most interested in feminist theory, as a teacher, scholar, and/or administrator, there are ways to express your appreciation for certain aspects of contemporary feminism (e.g., emphasis on coalition building, cultural critique, and shared governance) without using the politically loaded term *feminist* or naming particular theorists that hiring committee members may not like. Of course, if you have firm theoretical commitments and absolutely couldn't stand to work in a department that doesn't appreciate the theories and theorists that you love, you will want to just be honest about it and risk being eliminated from consideration.

You will also want to anticipate the types of questions you may be asked in informal interview situations (e.g., at lunch, during a walk from one university office to another, or right before or after a more formal interview activity). These questions may include queries about professors with whom you have worked, alumni from your graduate program, or well-known figures in your subarea. While such questions will most likely be a natural form of polite chitchat, sometimes they are used to gather information about how you work with others, how discrete you are, or where you are positioned theoretically. Knowing this, you will want to always be positive and professional—even if you can't stand the person about whom you're being asked. You should also be prepared for questions that you are not supposed to be asked, according to federal law, but may be asked out of sheer ignorance: questions about marital status, children, religion, ethnicity, etc. While you do not have to answer such questions, you also don't want to offend the person who has asked them. Consider answering in a way that brings the conversation back to professional criteria: "I understand why you might be concerned about _____; what I can tell you is that it is something that doesn't/wouldn't affect my teaching performance/scholarship/service."

Asking Your Own Questions

During any type of interview (whether by phone or in person), committees will expect candidates to ask intelligent questions. The best questions show not only that a candidate has been listening carefully during the interview process, but that he or she has researched the position, department, and school. Questions that are commonly asked by candidates in a preliminary interview for a tenure-track faculty position include:

- What approaches do your faculty typically use to teach literature/composition/creative writing?
- If I were hired by your department, what types of courses would I be teaching? What would a typical semester of teaching look like for me?
- What opportunities exist for proposing new courses?
- How does your department/school support the research activities of junior faculty?
- How much and what kind of service do junior faculty typically do during their probationary years?

Though it is typical for candidates to ask these types of questions in subsequent interviews (e.g., an on-campus interview), questions often become more specific later in the process. During a campus interview, it is considered appropriate to ask specific questions about what and how much you will be teaching, how many/what kinds of publications are required for tenure and promotion, and what committees you will likely be on as a new faculty member.

Offering Supplementary Materials

If you aren't asked for teaching materials or writing samples prior to an interview, it's appropriate to ask if you should (or could) bring such materials with you. Even if a search committee can't always take materials from all candidates (especially at convention interviews, where committee members would have to carry materials home in their suitcases), most interviewers appreciate the chance to look at sample syllabi or sample course descriptions (e.g., for courses you haven't taught but could teach) during an interview.

Interview Follow-up

After an interview, always write a thank-you note in which you express appreciation for the chance to interview, reiterate your qualifications, and express your continued interest in the position. Though some candidates do this over e-mail, hand-written letters on quality note cards or stationery make a bigger impression. (Just proofread carefully, since you won't have the benefit of your grammar or spell-checker!)

Beyond that, it is a matter of waiting. Generally, you will be told the time frame in which the department will be making decisions. If that time passes, it is appropriate to call or e-mail the chair of the committee or department to ask if they have made their decision and to reemphasize your interest in the position. Do not despair if you do not hear from a department right away—sometimes they have other candidates who have to visit; sometimes they make offers to other candidates that are rejected; or they have other issues that cause delay. If you are rejected, just cross the job off your list, see it as a chance to rehearse for a position that may turn out to be a better fit, and continue to search diligently.

Appendix B4: Helpful Job-Search Resources

Boufis, Christina, and Victoria C. Olsen, eds. *On the Market: Surviving the Academic Job Search.* New York: Riverhead Books, 1997.

Broughton, Walter, and William Conlogue. "What Search Committees Want."
    Profession 2001. New York: Modern Language Association, 2001. 39–51.

Carpini, Dominic Delli. "'Must Be Willing to Teach Composition': The Rhetoric
    and Practices of the Small College Job Search." *Composition Studies* 32.2
    (Fall 2004): 31–52.

Emmerson, Richard K. "When Do I Knock on the Hotel Room Door? The MLA
    Convention Job Interview." *ADE Bulletin* 111 (Fall 1995): 4–6.

Feirsen, Robert, and Seth Weitzman. *How to Get the Teaching Job You Want*.
    Sterling, VA: Stylus, 2000.

"Finding a Job in TESOL." TESOL Homepage < www.tesol.org >.

Formo, Dawn, and Cheryl Reed. *Job Search in Academe: Strategic Rhetorics for
    Faculty Job Candidates*. Sterling, VA: Stylus, 1999.

Gaines, Philip. "I've Looked at Jobs from Both Sides Now." *ADE Bulletin* 134–35
    (Spring–Fall 2003): 25–28.

Green, Eleanor H. "The Job Search: Observations of a Reader of 177 Letters of
    Application." *ADE Bulletin* 113 (1996): 50–52.

Gregory, Marshall. "How to Talk about Teaching in the MLA Interview." *ADE
    Bulletin* 111 (Fall 1995): 7–8.

Hume, Kathryn. *Surviving Your Academic Job Hunt: Advice for Humanities PhDs*.
    New York: Palgrave/Macmillan, 2005.

Kronenfeld, Jennie Jacobs, and Marcia Lynn Whicker. *Getting an Academic Job*.
    Thousand Oaks, CA: Sage, 1997.

Minter, Deborah, and Amy M. Goodburn. *Composition, Pedagogy, and the
    Scholarship of Teaching*. Portsmouth, NH: Boynton/Cook, 2002.

Moffatt, Courtney W., and Thomas L. Moffatt. *How to Get a Teaching Job*. Boston:
    Allyn and Bacon, 2000.

Musser, Joseph. "The On-Campus Interview." *ADE Bulletin* 111 (Fall 1995): 11–13.

Papp, James. "The Stars and Ourselves: An Ordinary Person's Guide to the
    English Market." *ADE Bulletin* 120 (Fall 1998): 2–9.

Parsons, Adelaide, ed. *The EFL/ESL Job Search Handbook*. Alexandria, VA: TESOL,
    1995.

Sadoff, Dianne F. "The MLA Interview: The Department's Perspective." *ADE
    Bulletin* 123 (Fall 1998): 11–12.

Showalter, English. *The MLA Guide to the Job Search*. New York: Modern Lan-
    guage Association, 1996.

Smith, Philip E. "Negotiating a Job Offer." *ADE Bulletin* 118 (Winter 1997): 33–34.

Thomas, Trudelle. "Demystifying the Job Search: A Guide for Candidates."
    College Composition and Communication 40 (1989): 312–27.

Two-Year College English Association (TYCA). "Guidelines for the Academic Preparation of English Faculty at Two-Year Colleges." November 2004.

Warner, Anne Bradford. "The Protocols of the Job Search." *ADE Bulletin* 114 (Fall 1996): 19–24.

Wilt, Judith. "How to Talk about Scholarship in the MLA Interview." *ADE Bulletin* 111 (Fall 1995): 9–10.

Authors

Photo: Andrew Harnack

Cindy Moore is assistant professor of English at Eastern Kentucky University, where she teaches a wide range of composition courses and helps coordinate department assessment efforts. Before moving to Kentucky, she directed writing programs in Indiana and Minnesota. It was as a program director, supervising and mentoring graduate teaching assistants, that she first began to think seriously about the importance of professional development. She is co-editor of *The Dissertation and the Discipline: Reinventing Composition Studies*, a collection of essays on issues related to dissertation research and writing, and *Practice in Context: Situating the Work of Writing Teachers*, a collection that highlights intersections between teaching, research, and theory for graduate TAs. She has also published numerous articles on writing, teaching, and mentoring.

Hildy Miller, associate professor of English and director of writing at Portland State University, teaches graduate courses and prepares students to teach both composition and literature. For years, she has been interested in the professional development of English students, mentoring and leading workshops for her department's students and giving papers and publishing in this area. Her chapter "Writing Beyond the Academy: Using Service-Learning for Professional Preparation of Undergraduates," which appeared in *Practice in Context: Situating the Work of Writing Teachers*, proposed one way to prepare English students to focus their job searches. She is co-editor, with Lillian Bridwell-Bowles, of the collection *Rhetorical Women: Roles and Representations.* Her other articles have appeared in various journals, including *College Composition and Communication* and *WPA: Writing Program Administration.*

This book was typeset in Shannon by Electronic Imaging.
The typefaces used on the cover were Hoefler Text and Text Engraved.
The book was printed on 50-lb. Williamsburg Offset paper by Versa Press, Inc.